CW01082483

FOOTBALL AGENT
EDUCATION

FOOTBALL AGENT EDUCATION

How to Become a Football Agent:
The Guide

2nd Edition

Foreword by
Robert Pires

Dr Erkut Sögüt LL.M.,
Jack Pentol-Levy, Charlie Pentol-Levy

Copyright © 2019 Dr Erkut Sögüt LL.M., Jack Pentol-Levy, Charlie Pentol-Levy

The moral right of the author has been asserted.

Apart from any fair dealing for the purposes of research or private study,
or criticism or review, as permitted under the Copyright, Designs and Patents
Act 1988, this publication may only be reproduced, stored or transmitted, in
any form or by any means, with the prior permission in writing of the
publishers, or in the case of reprographic reproduction in accordance with
the terms of licences issued by the Copyright Licensing Agency. Enquiries
concerning reproduction outside those terms should be sent to the publishers.

Matador
9 Priory Business Park,
Wistow Road, Kibworth Beauchamp,
Leicestershire. LE8 0RX
Tel: 0116 279 2299
Email: books@troubador.co.uk
Web: www.troubador.co.uk/matador
Twitter: @matadorbooks

ISBN 978 1838590 819

British Library Cataloguing in Publication Data.
A catalogue record for this book is available from the British Library.

Printed and bound by CPI Group (UK) Ltd, Croydon, CR0 4YY
Typeset in 11pt Gill Sans by Troubador Publishing Ltd, Leicester, UK

Matador is an imprint of Troubador Publishing Ltd

In recognition of all your support
and contribution to the book…

Robert Pires

With special thanks to…
Ilhan Gündoğan
Nassim Touihri
David Jackett
Harun Arslan
Loren Román García
Daniel Geey
Chris Wheatley
Rory Smith
Daniel Ross
Stéphane Ehrhart
Jörg Neubauer
Pere Guardiola
Paddy Dominguez
Matthieu Rios-Grossin
Costa Smyrniotis
Dee Hong
Yussif Alhassan Chibsah
Güllü Sögüt
Marco Vittorio Tieghi
Edoardo Revello

CONTENTS

Foreword by Robert Pires   xv
Introduction   xviii

Chapter One: Getting Into the Business   1
Internship or direct job application   2
A contact in the industry   4
Scouting   5
General business person   6
Conferences and events   7
Family member or friend   7
Buying an agency   9
The expert's view: Jack Pentol-Levy
       (Agent, Family & Football)   10

Chapter Two: Registering as an Agent   13
FIFA (Fédération Internationale
      de Football Association)   14
England: FA (Football Association)   15
Germany: DFB (Deutscher Fußball-Bund)   15
France: FFF (Fédération Française de Football)   16
Spain: RFEF (Real Federación Española de Fútbol)   16
Italy: FIGC (Federazione Italiana Giuoco Calcio)   17
Portugal: FPF (Federação Portuguesa de Futebol)   17
Netherlands: KNVB
      (Koninklijke Nederlandse Voetbalbond)   18
United States of America: USSF
      (United States Soccer Federation)   18
Turkey: TFF (Türkiye Futbol Federasyonu)   18
Australia: FFA (Football Federation Australia)   19

Chapter Three: The Work of a Football Agent   21
Understanding football   21
Networking   22
Who do you work for?   23
Location of work   24
Qualities of a football agent   24
Match days   26
The expert's view: Ilhan Gündoğan
      (Agent of Ilkay Gündoğan, Family & Football)   28

Chapter Four: Working with Players   30
Working with established professionals   31
Working with the friends and family of a player   31
Working with the spouse or partner of a player   32

Mental health   32
Clients as recruiters   34
The size of your client list   34
The expert's view: Nassim Touihri (Managing Director,
    Fair Play Career Management)   35

Chapter Five: Working with Youth Players   37
Handling youth players   38
Family of youth players   40
Sponsorships and boot deals   40
FIFA (Fédération Internationale
    de Football Association)   41
England: FA (Football Association)   41
Germany: DFB (Deutscher Fußball-Bund)   42
France: FFF (Fédération Française de Football)   43
Spain: RFEF (Real Federación Española de Fútbol)   43
Italy: FIGC (Federazione Italiana Giuoco Calcio)   43
Portugal: FPF (Federação Portuguesa de Futebol)   44
Netherlands: KNVB
    (Koninklijke Nederlandse Voetbalbond)   44
United States of America: USSF
    (United States Soccer Federation)   45
Turkey: TFF (Türkiye Futbol Federasyonu)   45
Australia: FFA (Football Federation Australia)   45
The expert's view: David Jackett (Global football
    consultant and agent)   47

Chapter Six:
    Working with Managers and Sporting Directors   49
Being the agent of a manager   50

Advantages of representing a manager   51
Young managers   52
Working alongside a sporting director   53
The expert's view: Harun Arslan
    (Owner, ARP Sportmarketing GmbH)   55

Chapter Seven: The Art of a Transfer   **56**
Preparation for the window   57
The strategy of the agent   58
Role of the agent in a transfer agreement   59
Mandates   61
Transfer fee   63
The personal side of a transfer   64
Winter transfer window: a 2018 case study   65
The expert's view: Dr Erkut Sögüt
    (Agent of Mesut Özil, Family & Football) 69

Chapter Eight: Loans and 'Free Agents'   **70**
What is a loan?   71
Advantages of loans   71
Options to buy   72
What is a 'free agent'?   73
Benefits and risks of 'free agency'   74
The expert's view: Loren Román García
    (Agent of Lucas Pérez, Family & Football) 76

Chapter Nine: Contracts   **77**
Representation Contract   77
Employment Contract   80
Contract renewals   81

Tripartite Representation Contract   82
The expert's view: Daniel Geey
      (Sports lawyer, Sheridans)   83

Chapter Ten: Social Media and Marketing   85
Image Rights Agreement   86
Boot deals   87
Endorsement deals   88
Social media   91
Personal brands   93
The expert's view: Chris Wheatley
      (Director, D2S Media)   94

Chapter Eleven: Working with the Media   96
Interviews and media work   97
Global sporting news outlets   98
Working with journalists   99
The expert's view: Rory Smith
      (Chief Soccer Correspondent, New York Times)   101

Chapter Twelve: The Off-Pitch Work of an Agent   103
Charity   103
Property   105
Tax   106
Wealth management and investments   106
eSports   108
The expert's view: Daniel Ross
      (Managing Partner, Ross Bennet Smith
      Chartered Accountants)   109

Chapter Thirteen:
    The Second Career of a Football Player   III
    (Written in conjunction with Stéphane Ehrhart of UEFA)
Facing the reality of retirement   112
Going about a player's second career   113
Football-related opportunities   115

Chapter Fourteen: A History of the Profession   118
The early years   119
Representation of football players   119
Recognition by FIFA   120
The Bosman ruling   121
The expert's view: Jörg Neubauer
    (Agent of Leon Goretzka and Kevin Trapp)   123

Chapter Fifteen: 'Show Me the Money'   125
Wages   125
Transfers   126
Other projects   128
Ownership and M&A (mergers and acquisitions)   128
The expert's view: Pere Guardiola
    (Director, Media Base Sports)   129

Chapter Sixteen: 'Global Views'   131
Australia: Paddy Dominguez
    (Owner, Republic Sports Management)   131
South America: Matthieu Rios-Grossin
    (Owner, Alinea Sports Management)   134

North America: Costa Smyrniotis
      (Director & Agent, Axia)   136
Asia: Dee Hong
      (Head of International Affairs, Footballade)   139
Africa: Yussif Alhassan Chibsah
      (CEO & Founder, Club Consult Africa)   140

Chapter Seventeen: Example Contracts   145
England: FA (Football Association)
      Representation Contract   145
Germany: DFB (Deutscher Fußball-Bund)
      Intermediary Application Form   149
Mandate for transfer   151
Premier League Employment Contract   156
Marketing deal   162

Conclusion   169

FOREWORD BY ROBERT PIRES

Looking back on my career, I was fortunate enough to be part of some legendary events and teams, from being a member of Arsenal's 'Invincibles', to World Cup victory with France in 1998. During such moments, it is sometimes difficult for players to take everything in and plan for the years ahead. It's easy for professionals in any sport or age-sensitive industry to forget that in a few years' time things won't be the same. That why, for me, although agents and intermediaries played an important part in my footballing career, they are equally (if not more) important now the glory years are over.

As I said, when you're playing week in, week out, the feeling is incredible, but once you retire players have to be aware that much of this stops. No longer are you signed to a playing contract with a club, and you soon realise that you have more free time despite still being young when compared to the retirement age of other professions.

This is why being represented by a forward-thinking agent is key for me. Having an agent who knows how to conduct business and create exciting opportunities both related and unrelated to football is so important.

Currently, I remain very close with my friends at Arsenal. Representing the club I once played for as an ambassador is something I'm proud to do. Whilst travelling the world on behalf of the Arsenal brand, I am able to engage with fans from different regions who I could never have met during my playing days. Also, it gives me the opportunity to increase my network of contacts across the globe, which could potentially be beneficial for projects that I am involved in. Whether you're a former player, an agent or a business person, this is the type of mentality that can be really advantageous to adopt. Aside from my ambassadorial role at Arsenal, I am also proud to have partnered with some great brands. Again, working alongside these international companies and taking part in legends tournaments gives me the chance to travel to places and meet people in a way that would otherwise not be possible.

I also now have more time to work with charities and be part of some amazing campaigns. I've realised that, with my platform, I have a unique opportunity to raise awareness and give back in a way that I never thought would have been feasible when I was growing up. There are so many remarkable organisations in France, the UK and all over the world that work tirelessly for far bigger causes than football. Of course, football is my love, my passion, but at the end of the day some things are bigger than sport. Representing these great charities and supporting their efforts is something I'm proud to do.

So, you may be thinking, where does the world of football agency and this book fit in with all I've said?

Without proper representation, it is difficult to organise and arrange of all the ventures and projects that footballers and ex-footballers are part of. Of course, agents are normally discussed when big transfers or contracts are negotiated, but that is no longer the area where I need a strong team supporting me.

Working with a small team of trustworthy, loyal and well-connected agents and business people is my preferred way of going about my career after football. Surrounding myself with like-minded people that I have faith in to help me grow, and also to have my back and be honest with me at all times. The best agents are the ones that know these types of relationships don't grow overnight. They are the ones that aren't focused on money and short-term success, but instead want to be working with me for years and years. Sharing is important, and you have to realise that in order to create and build successful projects, you need to work with like-minded people. In my experience, this always comes back to one key quality. Trust. Without a trusting relationship, success is not possible.

INTRODUCTION

Welcome to the second edition of *How to Become a Football Agent: The Guide*.

To those who have read the first edition, and to those who have not, we hope we can help you on your journey to becoming a football agent (or intermediary, as they are also called) and developing into one of the best in the business.

Whilst the core principles and content of the first edition remain in this book, we've added more chapters, more practical guidance and advice, and more views of top agents around the world. In addition, in order to give you a greater insight into the workings of the profession, example contracts pertinent to the world of football agency can be found towards the end.

Although this book aims to be of obvious benefit to football agents, both future and current, the guidance found within extends far beyond the game of football, or even sport. Whether it's tennis, rugby or basketball, the advice and know-how of dealing with professional athletes ultimately remains common. Similarly, the ideas relating to social media, marketing, and dealing with a client's friends and family remain relevant if you're dealing with musicians, actors or entertainers of any kind.

Back to the world of football, and our plan to change how the business looks on the outside, and operates on the inside, remains firm and resolute. There's no hiding that agents have a bad reputation in society, characterised as greedy business people that simply make a living off the talent of another individual, taking their share of the large amounts of money that players seem to earn.

Whilst this book will educate you on how to become a successful football agent, it additionally hopes to go some way towards getting rid of the aforementioned perception. Football agency is in many ways just like any other type of business or client-based service. Those who are out to get the best deal for themselves will eventually become unstuck, and those who try to secure the best deal for their client will prevail.

The book is structured in an easy-to-read format that hopes to provide these clear and constant messages and pieces of advice throughout. Being split into seventeen chapters, the second edition provides a more coherent journey from start to finish. By breaking each chapter down into smaller sections, we hope to enable you to look up a particular element of football agency with relative ease at a later date, and this makes it a book that will be accessible to anyone, at any time.

It is obvious that football agency inherently relies on the game of football and its developments. Living in a more interconnected world has meant that the sport has become far more international and increasingly globalised – consequently, the agency sphere reflects this. That is why there is a continual emphasis throughout the book on information that is pertinent to a range of the most popular footballing associations in the world, as well as presenting the current regulations compiled by FIFA (Fédération Internationale de Football Association).

Closely linked with the internationality of football is the eclectic mix of backgrounds, ages and locations of football agents. This again has resulted in the book attempting to constantly provide information that is relevant to a global audience – and remember, a football agent is no specific type of person; this profession is by no means restricted to any gender, age group or environment. This is why we've added a 'global views' chapter at the end of this edition which encompasses the opinions of leading figures in each of the main footballing continents.

Moreover, we have kept and expanded our 'experts' views' that conclude each chapter. Here, industry specialists relevant to the content of the chapter offer their experiences and thoughts on the subject, adding a personal touch and also providing you with skills, practical knowledge and wisdom that you can take with you on your journey as a football agent. These views do not come solely from agents; there are also opinions from those in professions such as law and journalism. This showcases how the agency business is not exclusive – you must work closely alongside other vocations to produce the best possible results.

As previously mentioned, the book hopes to inform you about how to become a successful and moral football agent. Yet, at the same time, reading this book alone will not ensure success in this tough industry. Being continuously active in establishing a network and always working hard and efficiently are characteristics that you must possess. Combined, these elements will give you the best chance in a difficult, yet intriguing and financially rewarding profession.

Football agency is thought of as being a closed industry, but with this edition we hope to show you that the industry *needs* well-informed and ethical intermediaries in order for the game to head in the right direction. According to FIFA's ITMS, there have been just under 70,000 international transfers worldwide since 2013, and given how there can be as many as three intermediaries involved (at least one representative each on the player, buying club and selling club sides) there is certainly room for you to come into this industry.

Who uses intermediaries?

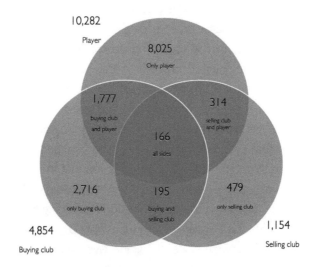

10,282
Player

8,025
Only player

1,777
buying club
and player

314
selling club
and player

166
all sides

2,716
only buying club

195
buying and
selling club

479
only selling club

4,854
Buying club

1,154
Selling club

Source: FIFA TMS – Intermediaries in International Transfer (2017 edition)

CHAPTER ONE

GETTING INTO THE BUSINESS

Before you can think about becoming a registered agent, you have to be in the business. For aspiring agents, this is often the most difficult aspect, and becoming an established intermediary is a notoriously hard process. The good thing, however, is that there is *no* set method, path or degree that you need to follow – leading football agents all have different backgrounds and stories that led them to enter their profession. Nevertheless, there are of course some more common routes into the football business. Whilst these do not guarantee success, they are certainly a very good place to start. Ultimately, how you become an established agent is up to how much you want it – those who work smart and dedicate the most time will prevail. This is a job that requires patience at the beginning in order to reap the rewards later.

Internship or direct job application

A common way into the footballing business is through applying for an internship or job, either towards the end of your studies or after completing them. Some of the agencies listed in the following table (and others too) *may* run internship schemes which they can employ from. Although internship schemes in general are naturally competitive, applying to as many as possible and trying to demonstrate your potential worth to them is pivotal. It is important to remember that gaining experience in the marketing or legal department of such firms can be just as valuable in the long term as working immediately alongside an agent. It may be that the contacts you make during your time at the company turn out to be crucial in your future career in the business. Even if you don't stay on after an internship or short mentoring agreement, it is crucial that during your time at an agency, you try as hard as you can to grow and enhance your network of contacts in order to acquire as much knowledge as possible.

Football agency	Clients represented
Family & Football	Mesut Özil, Ilkay Gündoğan, Shkodran Mustafi
GestiFute	Cristiano Ronaldo, James Rodríguez, Bernardo Silva
Stellar Football	Gareth Bale, Jesse Lingard, Jordan Pickford
Lian Sports	Miralem Pjanić, Kalidou Koulibaly, Marcos Alonso
Rogon Sportmanagement	Roberto Firmino, Thilo Kehrer, Tiémoué Bakayoko

Sports Entertainment Group	Memphis Depay, Stefan de Vrij, Kevin Strootman
SportsTotal	Toni Kroos, Marco Reus, Dayot Upamecano
Key Sports Management	Joe Gomez, Nathan Aké, Theo Walcott

Source: Transfermarkt (correct as of January 2019)

Of course, one naturally assumes that the most suitable type of internship is at a well-established football agency that has multiple top clients. However, from this presumption stem two common mistakes:

1. **Do your research.** Don't simply apply to the first handful of football agencies that come up when you search them! The top agents who try to do everything for their clients will no doubt need help if they want to expand to other players. Therefore, you should research agents who perhaps only have one or two players on their client list. Getting in touch with them can be just as effective as an internship at a large football agency. Although getting contact details of people like this is usually very tough, they may still have formed a company (and thus have an email address on their website or Transfermarkt page), or use networking websites such as LinkedIn. Similarly, they may be in attendance at network events and conferences (as will be discussed later in this chapter).

2. **Don't just apply to football agencies.** You can learn vital information about the world of football agency by interning or applying for a job at companies working in

football, but not explicitly from an agency perspective. For example, marketing and advertising firms, media companies, sports brands, clubs and many more interact with intermediaries constantly. From there, you might well be able to work your way into being in direct contact with an agent or agency.

A contact in the industry

Knowing somebody who is already connected to the footballing business is obviously an advantage that you should make the most of if you want to get into the industry. Such people can range from club employees (like managers or sporting directors) to existing agents, to friends of friends who know someone! It doesn't really matter how you find your connection, as long as it is done in good faith. When you're first introduced to this contact, certain things can be advised about how to present yourself:

1. **Be willing to learn.** Anybody who thinks they are already the perfect agent (or that it is easy to become one) will immediately be caught out by any established agent. You have to show that you are ready to learn and to do any task, as small as it may be.
2. **Be professional.** Whilst you want to convince this contact of your passion, you don't want to come across as overly eager or demanding. Agents are busy and often have little time, so make sure your words are smart and say what you want to say concisely. If you want this contact to give you the opportunity to

shadow them and accompany them to meetings, they have to be confident that your presence will be of benefit and not an inconvenience.

Scouting

A good way to go about getting your first client is by scouting youth and lower league fixtures. Often the first player you represent will be young and eager to work their way to the top divisions. Going to as many games as possible (and seeing a variety of teams) shows your desire to make your mark in the industry. Also, matches are a great networking opportunity. Not only can you meet the relatives of the player, but other agents, scouts and club officials from a variety of teams will also be present. You should always remain patient and professional, taking your time to research in order to make good decisions. For example, stopping in order to speak with a member of a player's family at the game is a great idea, as your relationship with the family is integral. Remember, if you want to work with youth players, there are certain rules and regulations you have to follow. For example, in England, you must not engage in any contact with a player regarding 'intermediary activity' before January of the year in which the player will celebrate their sixteenth birthday, and any contract with a minor must involve a parent or legal guardian signing off on the deal. These rules are addressed in more detail in Chapter 5.

In order to get to these games, you often have to request access through the clubs. That is why sometimes *not* registering before you get your first client can be advantageous, as clubs sometimes restrict the number of intermediaries attending certain youth games.

General business person

Many successful agents start off in mainstream professions, perhaps specialising in areas such as law, banking or teaching. Jobs like these, as well as so many others, are a great way into the business, as a player (and their representatives at the time) will always need the advice of specialists, for example in legal or financial matters. Consequently, there will be countless opportunities for professionals to make their way into the world of sport. This was the case with Jörg Neubauer, who started his career as a lawyer but became a prolific football agent, currently representing players such as Leon Goretzka and Kevin Trapp.

However, the legal profession is not alone in breeding intermediaries. Spielerrat, the company that represents Per Mertesacker, Serge Gnabry and Kai Havertz, was formed by three friends who previously worked at Adidas and decided to become football agents, with a strong network having been created as a result of their previous jobs. Furthermore, there are many business people that work closely with sport, whilst not actually being agents. Often, a business person can take care of a player's sponsorships or commercial dealings (or at least give advice on this subject) while continuing their day-to-day profession. Therefore, it is clear that there are numerous routes in the world of sports agency, with some ending in becoming an actual agent and others that just involve giving advice.

Conferences and events

Throughout the year, there are numerous events in the football business calendar that are worthwhile for aspiring agents to attend. Whilst not all of these will focus specifically on football agency, talks on marketing and finance within the sport can still provide crucial details that a good agent requires. The most well-known events include Leaders in Sport, Soccerex and the Wyscout Forum – these (amongst others) are well worth going to. Events tend to attract great speakers from a variety of sectors, and they can provide you with interesting and useful skills, information and experience. In addition, seminars and webinars, as well as lectures and other educational events, can be very beneficial.

But perhaps the greatest selling point for events such as these is that so many individuals working in the industry present at the same time, in the same place. This gives you the chance to meet new people and make worthwhile contacts, thereby expanding your network within a relatively short time. You never know when any contact could be helpful when applying for an internship or seeking advice in general. Also, it could be the case in years to come that, after establishing yourself as a top football agent, you are invited to talk at some of these events – this would be an offer that you really shouldn't turn down.

Family member or friend

If you are lucky enough to have a family member or friend who is an emerging footballing talent, then there is an obvious opportunity there. You may be fortunate enough to work with them directly in an agency capacity from the start. However, what is more often the case is that the player will already have an agent, and will entrust you with important everyday affairs. For example, you might seek commercial opportunities on their behalf, help manage their daily routine, or even just perform small tasks for them and their family. This is particularly the case when the agent has multiple clients or lives in a different country. Sometimes, this relationship between player and friend can develop into something much larger, as you are someone they trust and have known for a long time. This is how Nassim Touihri (the agent of Lukas Podolski) got into the business, as he started out as a friend of his future client, before forming his own agency (Fair Play Career Management) and taking Podolski with him.

Very common within the footballing world is that a relative of the player acts as their agent, with the following table noting some well-known examples. Whilst this may seem frustrating given the extremely slim chances of falling into this category, you should know that these family members will nearly always receive help and advice from qualified and educated agents behind the scenes. This means that, although you may not be listed as the official intermediary, you can still play a pivotal part and receive commission for your work.

Player / manager	Country	Agent	Agent's relationship to client
Sergio Ramos	Spain	René Ramos	Brother
Sami Khedira	Germany	Denny Khedira	Brother
Danny Welbeck	England	Chris and Wayne Welbeck	Brothers
Diego Simeone	Argentina	Natalia Simeone	Sister
Mats Hummels	Germany	Hermann Hummels	Father
Mario Götze	Germany	Jürgen Götze	Father
Lionel Messi	Argentina	Jorge Horacio Messi	Father
Álvaro Morata	Spain	Alfonso Morata	Father
Arjen Robben	Netherlands	Hans Robben	Father
Mauro Icardi	Argentina	Wanda Nara	Wife

Buying an agency

Perhaps the least common (and most expensive) way to get into the footballing business is to buy an existing and established agency. Although this is fairly rare, an example of such a takeover is not difficult to find in the news. In 2016, Chinese company Wuhan Double Co. Ltd purchased the sports agency Nice International Sports Ltd, in a deal that also involved a partnership with Pere Guardiola's firm, Media Base Sports. This is of course an extremely costly way into the industry; however, it is highly effective if the funds are available. Furthermore, despite it seeming unrealistic for many, if one were to get a job or internship at a large firm outside of the footballing business, a merger or deal with a football agency would not be totally impractical.

Summary

- The most important thing to remember is that there is no correct or incorrect way to become a football agent, as the top intermediaries come from all sorts of different backgrounds.
- If you are a student or young professional, getting experience through an internship at an agency can provide you with great insight and start your vital network in the business – but don't think this is an absolute necessity.
- For those already established in another profession, the world of football is within reach, as so many other industries such as law and finance have links to the sport.

The expert's view: Jack Pentol-Levy (Agent, Family & Football)

I am fortunate enough to have found myself working in the game of football, which I grew up loving from a young age. But when I started looking for internships during my second year at university, I really had no idea of what a football agent was, and certainly had no intention of ending up in this business!

My journey started when I was accepted into an internship programme at a large London-based agency, after applying to a vast array of firms and companies in the sports and entertainment worlds. Whilst I was excited to start the internship, I was soon disappointed with the very basic (and totally un-football-related) tasks I was given. That all changed when I met Dr Erkut Sögüt, who at the time was a consultant for the agency.

During my first few encounters with him, I didn't know who he represented at all. Erkut gave me some football scouting reports and research to do. I put absolutely everything into these tasks, and even though they were small I wanted to make sure that they were perfect when I presented them to Erkut.

I really only found out about Erkut's relationship with Mesut Özil when I accompanied him to the Emirates Cup that year. Although my internship soon came to an end (and I returned to university, where I actually studied abroad for the year), I kept in touch with Erkut, and met up with him a few times whenever I came back to London. Despite not feeling that significant at the time, these messages and brief meetups paved the way for my future job.

The next summer was when things really started to change. Erkut had left the agency where we'd met, and I began to shadow him every day. I cancelled all holidays and social plans, and essentially sacrificed any life I'd had beyond this work experience. In many of the meetings I attended I didn't even really say anything, as lots were in languages that I didn't speak, and at the time I was hugely inexperienced in this world!

Nevertheless, thanks to Erkut I met with clubs and other agents, went to commercial shootings, and ended up travelling to France to watch the European Championship in 2016, meeting lots of national team players and their families in the process. This allowed me to gain vast amounts of experience in a relatively short period of time, resulting in me working on Shkodran Mustafi's transfer from Valencia to Arsenal.

During the Euros I also met Ilkay Gündoğan, and subsequently made the suggestion that I could be of help to him in Manchester as I was still studying in Leeds at the time. As only Ilkay's cousin had moved with him from Germany, I started to do lots of small (but important) tasks for them, such as sorting bills and a house, organising the guests for the box, and liaising with the club in general. I actually ended up spending more time in Manchester than Leeds or London during this period!

However, once things had settled down in Manchester, I started to divide my week evenly between the three cities, travelling back and forth for games and important meetings. Once I finally completed my degree, I thought I was ready. But my mentor Erkut thought differently. Subsequently embarking on a law conversion has added another great quality and skill that I can take with me throughout my career.

CHAPTER TWO

REGISTERING AS AN AGENT

Throughout the last year, football's main governing body, the Fédération Internationale de Football Association (FIFA), has held several meetings in order to discuss the rules and regulations concerning football agents. The aim of these discussions is to see what can be improved and changed going forward. In Zurich in April 2018, a select group of agents were asked to attend a workshop in order to give their first-hand experience. The list of intermediaries present included our co-author Dr Erkut Sögüt, as well as Paddy Dominguez, Yussif Alhassan Chibsah and Costa Smyrniotis, all of whom form part of the 'global views' chapter of this edition.

Keeping updated with FIFA's meetings is important, as they will likely end in changes to the football agent regulations.

As things currently stand, the 2015 FIFA Regulations on Working with Intermediaries are the most relevant for agents looking to get licensed today. Whilst FIFA has its own set of rules that it requires a potential intermediary to follow, much power lies with the individual country's football association, as each nation has its own set of rules to be adhered to. This chapter explores the regulations and requirements for some of the main footballing federations, all of which have slightly different procedures. All of the necessary rules for registering as an intermediary (in any country) can also be found by reading the relevant association's rules on their website.

FIFA
(Fédération Internationale de Football Association)

As explained, the FIFA rules of 2015 regarding football intermediaries must be followed closely, and in conjunction with the footballing association you are part of. FIFA mentions the following requirements:

1. Any 'natural person' (individual human being) must have an impeccable reputation and sign the 'Intermediary Declaration for Natural Persons';
2. Any 'legal person' (private or public organisation) must have an impeccable reputation and sign the 'Intermediary Declaration for Legal Persons';
3. Intermediaries are to have no contractual relationship with leagues, associations, confederations or FIFA that could lead to a potential conflict of interests;
4. The contract of representation (between an intermediary and club or player) must be authenticated by the association.

England: FA (Football Association)

The process to become a licensed agent in England is certainly one of the easiest amongst the large footballing nations. All that is required is an initial £500 joining fee, a renewal fee of £250 each year, and proof that you do not have a criminal record, in accordance with the 'Test of Good Character and Reputation'. Finally, you must prove that you are not employed by any club and do not have any shares in a club within England.

Germany: DFB (Deutscher Fußball-Bund)

Registering as an agent under the guidelines of the DFB is simple, yet there are different levels of registration. As a basic intermediary, all that is needed is the completed application form (as found on their website and in Chapter 17 too); a €500 fee, of which you are notified via an invoice from the DFB accountancy department; and a signature to declare that you have no contractual ties with other associations that could lead to a conflict of interests. The DFB also offers preregistration. Although the signing-up process is very similar (application form, €500 fee and signed declaration document), the main difference is that the club (or player) isn't legally obliged to ensure that the intermediary is registered, whereas they have to provide evidence that they are officially an agent if they are only 'registered' instead of 'preregistered'.

Additionally, when a player signs a new contract at the club, the Representation Contract is mutually terminated, and a new contract is signed between the agent and the club. Afterwards, the player re-signs with the agent. Whilst this may sound complex, it is done for tax purposes for the club.

France: FFF (Fédération Française de Football)

The French Football Association updated its rules and regulations for registering as an intermediary in 2011. There are now two principal examinations that you are required to take, each comprising twenty questions. The first exam tests your legal knowledge and knowledge of tax and insurance, and includes a case study or practical question at the end. The second examination is more specific to the world of football. Candidates are questioned on the football rules and regulations in France as well as internationally.

Spain: RFEF (Real Federación Española de Fútbol)

The enrolment process in Spain is vastly different to the other leagues. Firstly, an applicant must submit a written application to the general secretariat of the RFEF, and if this request is accepted, the candidate will be summoned to interview (which can be conducted via a video-chat service). After passing the interview, the rest of the procedure resembles those of many other associations. Each aspiring intermediary must have an impeccable reputation, pay the obligatory fee to the RFEF, and sign the 'Code of Conduct' forms.

Italy: FIGC (Federazione Italiana Giuoco Calcio)

Unlike Spain, in Italy the route to becoming a registered agent is simple, and greatly resembles the methods of other associations. In addition to the declaration of 'professional fairness', one must not have committed sports fraud or have a criminal record. Furthermore, there is a payment to the FIGC that is valid for one year, after which it is required (if still wanted to be an agent) to re-register via a fast-track process (unless any amendments have to be added to the aforementioned declaration). Alternatively, an intermediary may register before the FIGC only in the event of a specific representation contract's filing.

As of very recently, there has been an important addition to the rules in Italy. Now, an agent must pass a qualifying exam in order to be a fully licensed intermediary.

Portugal: FPF (Federação Portuguesa de Futebol)

The Portuguese footballing body has implemented a straightforward process to becoming a registered agent. Along with the relevant identification documents, those wanting to become a registered intermediary have to send in proof of no criminal record, as well as a declaration of solvency and a confirmation of no other contracts that could lead to a conflict of interests. In addition to the FPF focusing on the finances of a potential agent (an applicant is also required to have a civil liability insurance policy and a regularised tax situation), the association is keen on agents having a good reputation, which is frequently reassessed.

Netherlands: KNVB
(Koninklijke Nederlandse Voetbalbond)

With regards to the system in the Netherlands, you have to provide a signed 'intermediary statement', along with the other standard documents confirming your name and good character. The registration fee is determined by the KNVB on February every year (and is announced as such), and your intermediary licence expires yearly on 31 March following registration. In order to become a valid agent once again, you have to pay the renewal fee.

United States of America: USSF
(United States Soccer Federation)

The registration process for becoming an agent in the United States is very similar to that in England. To go along with the completed Intermediary Registration Form, an initial $400 must be paid to the governing body, and then a renewal fee of $50 each year. Moreover, you are subject to a background check and must not be employed by FIFA or any other governing body or national association. The USSF (much like the German association) also offers preregistration, which entitles you to the same benefits with increased efficiency in transfers and contracts.

Turkey: TFF (Türkiye Futbol Federasyonu)

The Turkish Federation of Football (TFF) set out its regulations for football agents (also known as 'managers' in Turkish, deriving from the word **menajer**) in June 2015. Prior to these changes, Turkish applicants had to sit the same exam as other European/FIFA nations. Under the new rules, an agent must be a 'natural person', but can also organise their work through a company, although even then only the registered intermediary can act as such. Article 4 of the regulations rules that you no longer have to be a Turkish citizen, have a legal place of residence or a work permit to be legally registered.

Like in other nations, club officials, players and managers can't be agents, or be part of an agency. On this note, individuals must declare that they comply with the criteria of the test of good character for agents upon registration, and they must confirm that they continue to meet those criteria every time they carry out intermediary activity in relation to a transaction. This is reiterated in the signed letter stating that the agent will carry out deals under the rules and principles of FIFA and TFF.

The evaluation committee of the TFF will then review the application, a process that occurs only in December and May of every year. If approved, an applicant must attend a 'football agent education workshop' (or seminar), whereby they will become a licensed agent. In addition, the agent has to pay the registration fee every year, and non-compliance will result in the suspension of the licence.

Australia: FFA (Football Federation Australia)

The process in Australia is somewhat similar to that in Germany. You can act as a valid intermediary via one of two different processes of registration. Firstly, the more traditional route is that of 'pre-lodgement'. This method is in essence the same as getting registered in England (for example), due to how straightforward it is. Simply fill out the pre-lodgement form, send the necessary documents to the FFA by post, and pay the fee of either $250 (plus GST) or $500 (plus GST) depending on when you sign up. Alternatively, the other way of becoming registered is that the player or club you are representing enrols you as an intermediary once you start to engage in a transaction.

The benefit of using the pre-lodgement process is that you appear as a licensed agent on the FFA's website, meaning players and clubs alike will see your name if they use this list when looking for representation.

Summary

- Making sure that you are legally registered as an agent in the appropriate association is key, and there are harsh implications if the rules are not abided by.
- If you are the agent of a player transferring to another country, you may or may not have to register as an intermediary in the new country as well – this depends on the exact rules set out by each federation.
- For additional information on the associations already mentioned, as well as details of registering in other countries, visit the website of the relevant federation.

CHAPTER THREE

THE WORK OF A FOOTBALL AGENT

Despite there being a certain perception by fans that the football agent profession is simple and straightforward, it is a job that requires you to be active all the time and encompasses different tasks each and every day. As in nearly all careers, the busier you are, the better, as more work correlates to more clients and thus more income! There is no fixed daily routine for a football agent, although intermediaries working for an agency will have more structure, but even so life in this profession is unpredictable and exciting.

Understanding football

Having a good knowledge of players, clubs and leagues is a very important aspect of the profession. Understanding which type of player goes to which type of club is often overlooked as a skill, but agents must always think ahead. Monitoring the performances of certain players and clubs can be helpful, as well as keeping an eye on the appointment of back-room staff and club officials. There are some helpful tools to keep yourself updated on the latest in football, including Transfermarkt, ESPN and sports newspapers and magazines, whilst paid services like Wyscout are also extremely useful. Making notes and jotting down ideas about players that you represent (or know the agent of) is certainly advisable, as it may be relevant for a future deal. Similarly, a 'scouting report', or just noting down thoughts for potential players for a club that you have a contact at, is also very useful, especially if you are to meet with a sporting director or club official.

Networking

Your network is your net worth! Networking is vital in the football business. The bigger and better your network, the more likely you are to succeed in the industry. Whilst building a wide-reaching network may seem like a daunting task, there are many ways to do this, through sporting events such as Soccerex and the Wyscout Forum, and just generally trying to be proactive. You have to utilise your contacts well, and find out what *you* can offer, too – business often centres around exchanging favours and working together. Use your knowledge of the football industry to identify gaps in the market, players without agents or players needing new clubs, and then try to work your way into a position where you can make a difference.

However, establishing the network is only one part of the process. To have a strong network requires you to keep in touch with everyone, even when there doesn't seem to be a need to. This could be done by email, text messages or phone calls, but perhaps more effectively by setting up face-to-face meetings. These can take the form of an invitation to a match day, or organising a time to catch up at an office, hotel, restaurant or café. Overall, the importance of building and effectively using a network cannot be underestimated – it forms the basis of your everyday actions and will ensure success in the industry.

Who do you work for?

The answer to this is simple: the player. Whilst you may see large football agencies with a vast array of clients, each player will have an agent within that agency who deals with them directly.

Nevertheless, a key distinction between agents is whether you work as part of a big agency or are more independent, and there are advantages to both. By being part of a large agency, you have the benefit of great resources, a vast network and often good player-recruitment power. Furthermore, as an employee, there are certain employment privileges that you are entitled to, and you have the security of a job.

However, being independent from an agency certainly has its benefits too. You definitely have more freedom, and don't have the pressure of having to be answerable to a superior. In addition, your hours and schedule can be more flexible, and you can go about your business in a far more unrestricted manner.

Location of work

Being a football agent is a job that requires you to be active, and thus normally involves much travelling. As already mentioned, those working as part of an agency will certainly have more structure to their routine, and consequently will have a desk or office from which they are based. However, for those that are independent, your headquarters are everywhere and change every day! Interaction with your client is key, and therefore visiting them, either at their house or at the training ground, and accompanying them to commercial shootings, are of paramount importance. Most agents will have a certain location in which they prefer to meet business people and other agents. Sometimes a low-key restaurant or café can provide the perfect setting to talk over deals, but upscale hotels and eateries are also popular amongst intermediaries, particularly when hosting significant or foreign guests. Therefore, it is clear that, as with most aspects of the business, there is really no fixed formula and it greatly depends on you as an individual and the situation you find yourself in.

Qualities of a football agent

All football agents have their own style and their own way of doing things. However, there are certain characteristics that many share, and that aspiring agents should try and adopt. Amongst the most important are loyalty and trust. In order for a client to allow you to negotiate deals on their behalf, they have to trust you and believe that you'll do what is best for them, and not act selfishly. Some agents, when negotiating contracts with clubs, ask what their commission will be first. Good agents do not do this; they get the best deal possible for the player and then work out their commission. You always have to work based on the best interests of your player, as you are representing them. Especially when dealing with younger players, this includes gaining the trust and respect of their parents, who are essentially allowing you to work closely alongside their child.

In addition, football agents have to be hard-working and willing to sacrifice. No agent has it easy from the start, and you have to work as hard as possible in order to be successful in this tough industry. Make the most of every meeting, every contact and every day – if you do, it will put you on the right path. Be sure to create the next opportunity for your client, and don't just wait around for somebody to approach you! At the end of the day, the best agents are the ones managing everything for their player – from contracts to sponsorships, you should be the one making things happen. This doesn't mean you shouldn't let others in, however, as utilising your network and experts in different fields is a key skill too.

Also, many top football agents have the ability to speak more than one language. Knowing a second language gives you a better opportunity to do business in the country (or countries) in which your second language is spoken. Furthermore, before travelling to any other country on business, you should try and research the key customs and be respectful of the traditions of that culture. For example, in Japan you must always give and receive business cards using both hands and ensure the card is turned towards the receiver. Not following this protocol is seen as rude and disrespectful. In general, travelling is a fundamental part of being a football agent, and you have to be prepared to spend time away from your home. But at the same time, this is an aspect of what makes the profession so enjoyable and interesting – you get the chance to travel all across the world and interact with a variety of people.

The most important thing to remember when working as a football agent is to always be prepared. Your day will mostly comprise of meetings with a range of different people, perhaps spanning various industries, and therefore it is for you to be ready for the day ahead. This includes being equipped with a phone and laptop (with chargers), as well as a notepad. Keeping a copy, either digitally or in writing, of what has been agreed in your meetings helps you keep track of all your business. As with any profession, preparation and organisation are key factors in success.

Match days

Some of the most important parts of each week are match days, occurring on the weekends and often midweek too. Depending on the exact nature of your relationship with the player, motivational conversations before the game can be greatly beneficial, and, given the importance of your client's performance in aiding your own career, every little you can do to help them has to be done. Regarding the logistics of the match day, most top players normally have an allocation of two tickets, although it is becoming more and more common for players to have access to a box. This would normally come in the form of their own suite, as evidenced at Manchester City, where the Colin Bell Stand is home to ten squad member boxes including those of Raheem Sterling, John Stones and Leroy Sané. However, these private areas can also be shared between players.

In either case, as the agent, it is your responsibility to organise the guests. Though some of the player's family will request access to the tickets, it is crucial to find the balance between them and business guests. Allocating the tickets between friends, family, commercial partners, potential partners and other agents in the business is key. To help with this, you should always keep in mind that it is your job and you are in the business side of football, so try to treat these match days as potential gateways to further deals. Even though matches are ninety minutes long, for agents the match day lasts the whole day and often the surrounding days too! You have to meet with guests and get them to the stadium a couple of hours before kick-off, and stay with them after the game, too – these are great times to talk business. But if they are flying in especially for a match, then you should offer to meet the day before or after the game day. As previously mentioned, games can be twice a week for your client, and as an agent you will probably also be invited into the boxes of other players who have an agent that you're close with, and also sometimes the director's box – so make sure you're committed to long hours! Furthermore, as is discussed in Chapter 12, match days also provide a great opportunity to host charitable guests and offer them the opportunity to meet your client and other players after the game.

Summary

- The football industry is non-stop – you must remember that there is always work to do, and those that work hardest and smartest will succeed the most.
- Generally, work in this profession is unpredictable, and that is why flexibility (in addition to preparation and organisation) is so crucial – particularly when dealing with numerous clients, or in overseas business interests.
- Despite the difficulties you may face, the fact that every day brings a new challenge to overcome is not only exciting but also really rewarding and something you should relish.

The expert's view: Ilhan Gündoğan (Agent of Ilkay Gündoğan, Family & Football)

With regards to the day-to-day work of a football agent, I know that some people believe it is so easy that anyone can do it. However, the truth is very far from this. The content of my job varies greatly each day and is also dependent on the time of year.

During the season my focus is mostly on the management of my nephew, Ilkay Gündoğan. This involves speaking to him on a regular basis and providing him with support and encouragement when necessary, as well as motivating him so that he keeps playing to the best of his ability. Moreover, I am there for anything he needs – similar to a concierge service. Finally, leading up to each match day, I coordinate with the guests that will attend the game – inviting key people in the business, as well as off-the-field individuals from brands and companies, is important.

Seeking and managing commercial deals for my player [see Chapter 10] is likewise a big part of my job. This involves meeting with current partnered brands on a regular basis, as well as seeking new possible endorsements. Most importantly, being available twenty-four hours a day, seven days a week, is something you must be prepared for if you wish to be successful in this business – because if you aren't, then somebody else will be.

CHAPTER FOUR

WORKING WITH PLAYERS

Sometimes, it can be difficult to find the correct balance between managing the business and personal sides of a player's life, as the two are so often intertwined. You need to make sure they represent themselves in the best possible way, but don't want to seem overbearing. There is no set procedure for how to best work alongside a player, and it greatly depends on the age, fame and personality of your client. Nevertheless, there are certain actions that are advised when dealing directly with a player, and equally there are some things better left undone. The way in which you choose to work with a client is also impacted by your own situation. This relies on not only how many clients you have, but if those relationships are simply mandates for a transfer or full-time representation, and whether you are employed by an agency or working independently.

Working with established professionals

With a client who is already fairly well known, it is important for you to make the most of both their footballing ability and their sponsorship potential, especially when they are at the pinnacle of their career. When dealing with an established professional, it can be really beneficial to have a long-term plan, as well as backup plans for safety. Although football is unpredictable, making connections with a range of clubs that could in the future offer a big transfer for your player is characteristic of a good agent. Regarding your player's personal life, it is crucial to find a balance. Whilst you have their best intentions and interests at heart, being too controlling and overbearing is not the way forward, and agents who are will not last long in the business. Ultimately, this is something that you learn along the way, and that varies player by player.

Working with the friends and family of a player

Despite often not being thought of as truly significant, knowing how to work alongside the friends and family of your client is certainly something of importance. Often, those who are close to the player are the people who can influence them the most, and therefore working with them is pivotal. Of course, this may be a legal obligation with the parents of a youth player, but even a famous footballer will always take advice from those closest to them. Consequently, as an agent, you should keep close family and friends aware of your intentions, both with the player's football career and with their commercial agreements. Also, if other players can see you're the type of agent that really interacts and works with the friends and family of a client, then that can only paint you in a positive light. But of course, this should not be the main motivating factor!

Working with the spouse or partner of a player

A difficult situation that nearly all football agents face at some point is when their player enters a relationship. The influence of a spouse or partner is obvious, as the 'other half' of a footballer plays a crucial decision-making role. For example, the career of a player's partner may impact the likelihood of them transferring to another city or country, and often, if a couple have young children, this too can make moving more difficult. Therefore, it is pivotal that you, as the agent, recognise the personal needs of your client, but at the same time make sure that they are fully aware that they have to make the most of their career whilst there is the possibility to do so.

Mental health

Something that many fans don't fully realise is the pressure that footballers are under. Of course, most fans point to the money and recognition as the remedies for any time that a player may feel down or depressed, but your role as agent allows you to be much more than simply a middleman who gets your clients deals. Stepping out in front of thousands (and a TV audience of millions) and playing the sport you love as a profession is something that so many kids dream of growing up to do, but behind the scenes the realities are different. Established professionals are still only in their twenties, and mentally grow up and develop in a public environment that is relatively abnormal. The eyes of countless people are constantly on them, and social media acts as a conduit for abuse and harsh criticism. Moreover, knowing that inevitably your career could come to an end following a single challenge, and is likely over once you reach your thirties, can only be daunting. Not to mention the 'footballer lifestyle' that many players feel pressured to act out, and the times where you could be dropped from the squad or transferred out to a completely new country. All of this takes some sort of a toll on any human being, and part of your job is to recognise that. Simply being there and offering support for your client is an easy way to help them, and this is why having a good relationship with their family and friends is crucial. In addition, lots of teams are starting to employ staff to talk with players about some issues, but suggesting that your client sees someone independently may not be a bad idea either.

Unfortunately, recent news has only proved the importance of this. The issue of racism remains rife in modern football, and many players from a range of backgrounds, religions and races are subject to this horrific verbal (and sometimes physical) abuse. Ensuring that your client chooses to react in the right way is crucial. It is obviously a very personal matter and each player will have their own feelings and thoughts about it, and it is for you to support and advise accordingly. Partnering with charities looking to combat racism and discrimination, and using the player's platform to try and push for change, are paths taken by lots of footballers who are subject to this mistreatment.

Clients as recruiters

Aspiring agents often ask how to expand their client list after they have managed to get their first player. A good answer to this is the player themselves! Whilst using your client as a full-time recruiter is a bit much, players do talk to each other, whether at training or during free time. Therefore, if you know a player at your client's club has no agent or just split from their agent, then asking your player to put in a good word is quite normal in the agency world. Similarly, if you know that a player is looking to move, you could ask your client to help you get in touch with their agent about helping to conduct a transfer. Moreover, if you find yourself representing a player who plays at an international level for their country, then the same logic applies!

The size of your client list

Much like how to deal with your player, it is important to find the right balance between having too many and only a few clients. Although it may seem financially beneficial to have lots of clients, it is difficult to manage numerous players at the same time, especially when you're fairly inexperienced as an agent. Nevertheless, multiple clients tend to mean multiple sources of income, and therefore it is advised that you choose perhaps a handful of clients who have great potential. The fact that having various clients is time-consuming and fairly difficult stresses the importance of getting on with your players' families and friends, as they can help out with some of the smaller and more day-to-day tasks.

Summary

- You must always aim to find the appropriate balance between the business and personal aspects of your job – this is something only you can discover as you go along.
- A good way to ensure success is to always be open and communicate frequently with your client, as this proves to them your honesty and transparency.
- The decisions that you make with regards to clients and other aspects of the profession are without doubt important, but at the same time they are not permanent – always be sure to review and improve the choices you have made.

The expert's view: Nassim Touihri (Managing Director, Fair Play Career Management)

As an agent, it is crucial to have a good, strong relationship with your player. For me, this is established through trust and honesty at all times, and these are the most important characteristics of an intermediary who is successful in their field of work. Although this is easier said than done, in my experience there are ways of achieving this type of relationship with a player. You must always be willing to help them in their personal life when they come to you for advice, but at the same time do not try to interfere in matters that simply don't concern you – finding the balance is key. Remember, not only do you have to protect your player from others, but you must also protect them from themselves, as they can endanger their own career at any point.

Regarding the business aspect of the player–agent relationship, you have to be constantly thinking ahead and making smart plans. At the end of the day, as an intermediary you are responsible for all of your client's interests and you have to be both managing their football career and making preparations for their post-playing career – this is the sign of a good agent.

Personally, I was a little lucky in that Lukas Podolski has been my close friend since we were young kids at school. But, at the same time, I had to work incredibly hard and my role today was not given to me because of our friendship. Even when I did not officially represent Lukas, I was always by his side giving advice in both personal and contractual matters. Eventually, our relationship evolved into what it is today. As I said (and will always say), trust and honesty are the qualities that breed success in this business.

CHAPTER FIVE

WORKING WITH YOUTH PLAYERS

Stemming from FIFA regulations, there are very strict rules concerning agents working with youth players and minors. Much like the registration processes (see Chapter 2), the football associations all have slightly different rules, yet they are all focused on protecting the young players, with strict punishment (for agents and clubs) if these regulations are not adhered to. With the growth of youth footballing talent around the world leading to more scouts and more transfers, there is increasing monitoring of these policies by football federations.

In recent news, it is clear to see the implications of not following the rules closely. In February 2019, Chelsea was handed a transfer ban (for two windows) for breaching the regulations with regards to minors on twenty-nine separate occasions. Whilst the club has since appealed the ban, it only goes to show the severity of the mishandling of youth players. Yet such neglect of youth regulations is not confined to England, with Barcelona, Real Madrid and Atlético Madrid all receiving transfer bans in the last few years due to not following the relevant policies. Therefore, these rules have to be followed closely, regardless of the country or association, and make sure that you secure the dates and a copy of any contract signed by a youth player for later reference in case of any disputes as to age or legality. In addition to knowing the rules with regards to youth players, it is also crucial to understand how to work with such players, as you often have to adopt a different approach.

Handling youth players

For a young player, the agent should on the one hand be encouraging and nurturing of their talent, whilst at the same time casting an eye to the future. With players that are still in school, it is partially your responsibility as the agent to make sure they continue to be educated and do schoolwork. As a result, you may work closely with the schools and academies, who are required to have their own education officer(s) to manage such affairs, as the teachers and coaches form an important part of a player's early career. Such a point is validated by how Mesut Özil, Manuel Neuer and Leroy Sané all went to the same school and later to the Schalke 04 Academy. In addition, in case of serious injury (or any other reason), it is vital that the player can rely on an education for their future.

With regards to on-pitch matters, having a youth player signed to a big club (i.e. a Premier League team) doesn't necessarily mean success. A couple of common scenarios normally arise with players signed to the academies of top teams:

1. **Fringes of first team.** Of course, if you're working with a youth player who is on the border of making it to the first team, this is an incredible position to be in. It would only take a couple of injuries to more senior players, or perhaps cup competitions, to see the player get some playing time. From here, your job is to keep the player grounded and remained focus on working hard.

2. **Not getting much playing time.** Given the resources of top-tier clubs, they often have a large number of young players on their books. Whilst being signed to one of these is certainly a huge accomplishment, if they aren't playing then perhaps action has to be taken. Securing a loan deal to a lower league team will ensure playing time, and at this stage in a young player's career that is really important. Obviously, each scenario varies case by case, and it is about adapting to the situation smartly.

According to FIFA's Transfer Matching System (TMS), age appears to be a crucial factor in the frequency of intermediaries being involved in transfers on behalf of the player. Players under the age of eighteen represent a higher percentage of intermediary involvement in international transfers than any other age group, therefore showcasing the large market there is in agency work with youth players.

Family of youth players

Even more important than with professional players, having a good relationship and working directly with (normally) the parents of youth players is crucial. Firstly, this is a legal necessity in some countries, as a legal guardian has to sign off on the documents. But, furthermore, the parents are (generally) the ones who have since a young age taken their child to training, bought them boots and apparel, and cared for them in all aspects – therefore you simply can't expect to be able to 'take over' and be a sole decision-maker. From a transfer to a boot deal to social media, consulting the parents on every issue and decision is pivotal and a key part of your job.

Sponsorships and boot deals

Nearly every young player dreams of their big boot deal with a top sports brand, and this is something that you have to try and deliver. Although large endorsements don't often come with youth players (unless they are an elite talent), you still have to try and get the player on the books of some sporting brand. Even if it is initially just free gear and equipment and a very small fee, this is definitely a great start. When you approach a sports brand about a young player, they will look into their on-pitch statistics, as well as their social media. This is why suggesting to the player that they have a professional social media presence is crucial. Posting pictures from games and training sessions, instead of things that are inappropriate, is something you have to work together with their parents to talk about.

FIFA
(Fédération Internationale de Football Association)

But, before *any* work with minors can be done, you have to be registered. The governing body of football has a fixed set of guidelines regarding minors that must be obeyed by all agents within the 211 member countries:

1. Players can only be transferred internationally over the age of eighteen;
2. The only exceptions (to Rule 1) are those concerning familial, academic or geographical issues – however, a transfer of a player aged sixteen to eighteen can take place within the European Union (EU) or European Economic Area (EEA), whilst arranging education and accommodation;
3. The Players' Status Committee has the power to rule on disputes and impose punishments if these regulations are not abided by.

England: FA (Football Association)

The rules in relation to intermediaries and youth players in England have recently been updated and are naturally rigorous. The English footballing body has declared that an agent must not engage in any contact with a player regarding 'intermediary activity' before January of the year in which the player will celebrate their sixteenth birthday. This rule is coupled with the fact that any contact with a minor has to be agreed and signed off on by the player's parent or legal guardian. Furthermore, an agent can't receive commission from a deal until the player is eighteen. However, as you'll know, lots of top youth talent sign professional contracts long before they reach this age. If this occurs, it is **sometimes** the case that the commission can be backdated upon the signing of a new contract once the player is over the age of eighteen.

Germany: DFB (Deutscher Fußball-Bund)

In Germany, the rules on the representation of youth players are often thought of as fairly controversial. The more straightforward aspect of this set of regulations is that German labour law instructs that those aged between seven and eighteen are not eligible to sign a deal without the consent of a parent or legal guardian. Yet the German rules become more complicated with the possibility of signing a **Fördervertrag** – an agreement by both parties (player/legal guardian and club) to place additional years on the typical three-year contract. This, of course, goes some way towards contradicting the FIFA rules, thus legal ambiguity remains over the issue. Therefore, this stresses the importance of making sure, as the representative of the young player, that you keep all the necessary paperwork and check all the times and dates are correct. Moreover, the aforementioned rules about the backdating of commission can sometimes occur in Germany too.

France: FFF (Fédération Française de Football)

The FFF requires a lawyer or legal consultant to sign the Representation Contract between the agent and the player, if the latter is a minor. In addition, an intermediary may not receive money (or collect any financial rewards) for representing a youth player, and any agent found breaching this rule would be subject to punishment by the federation.

Spain: RFEF (Real Federación Española de Fútbol)

The RFEF restates the rules given by FIFA in regard to minors. It reiterates how the international transfer of players is only allowed when the player reaches the age of eighteen, yet there are exceptions to this. These exceptions mirror those given earlier in the chapter relating to location, education and accommodation.

Italy: FIGC (Federazione Italiana Giuoco Calcio)

The Italian footballing association details the rights of young players and has different rules for different age groups. At the age of fourteen, a player can register with a professional club in an arrangement that ties them to it until the end of the season commencing the year they turn nineteen (they are the so-called *giovani di serie* players). During the last month of this last season, the player can be hired on a contract that must not exceed three years, but the club of which they have been part since they were fourteen has priority over other clubs. In addition, clubs can offer a *giovane di serie* player an Employment Contract once they turn sixteen. Players have the right to sign an Employment Contract if a specific number of appearances with the first team have been played. Of course, these rules and regulations have to be followed closely alongside FIFA's rules, and always check the relevant association's website for further clarity.

Portugal: FPF (Federação Portuguesa de Futebol)

Regarding the relationship between minors and intermediaries, the FPF simply adheres to the rules set out by FIFA. It declares that agents cannot act on behalf of underage athletes. This regulation is reinforced by Portugal's domestic law, which forbids underage representation and exploitation.

Netherlands: KNVB
(Koninklijke Nederlandse Voetbalbond)

According the Dutch rules and regulations, agents are not permitted to do any work (or related activities) with a player who is younger than fifteen years and six months old. In addition, you cannot receive any payment for the representation of a minor. The KNVB defines a minor by using whatever is the earliest date: that of the signed agreement of a playing contract/transfer, or the starting date of the playing contract/transfer.

United States of America: USSF (United States Soccer Federation)

The USSF regulations differ slightly from those presented by FIFA. The second aforementioned FIFA ruling (concerning the EU or EEA) is not relevant to the USA given that it is not part of either organisation. Instead, the USSF presents some of its own regulations regarding the transfer of a minor. Depending on the exact situation the player finds themselves in, the necessary documentation may include birth certificates or proof of parental residence and work, as well as various other papers and records.

Turkey: TFF (Türkiye Futbol Federasyonu)

The TFF also has strict rules on underage representation, in the hope of preventing the exploitation of youth players. Under Article 14 of the regulations, youth players are allowed to work with agents, but the agent cannot take a fee or payment if a transfer is conducted. Furthermore, an agent is forbidden to sign an agreement with a youth player under the age of fifteen, with the punishment being the revocation of the agent's intermediary licence.

Australia: FFA (Football Federation Australia)

The FFA doesn't add much to the FIFA regulations with regards to the representation of minors, thereby reiterating the already mentioned rules. They reiterate that you are not allowed to be remunerated by a club or a player where the deal involves a player aged under eighteen.

Most expensive teenagers (aged eighteen and under)

Player	Age	Transfer	Fee (M £)
Martin Ødegaard	16	Strømsgodset IF → Real Madrid (Castilla)	£2.52
Theo Walcott	16	Southampton → Arsenal	£9.45
Pietro Pellegri	16	Genoa → Monaco	£18.81
Fabricio Coloccini	17	Boca Juniors → AC Milan	£6.75
Jadon Sancho	17	Manchester City → Borussia Dortmund	£7.05
Gareth Bale	17	Southampton → Tottenham Hotspur	£13.23
Alexandre Pato	17	Internacional → AC Milan	£19.8
Antonio Cassano	18	Bari → AS Roma	£25.65
Wayne Rooney	18	Everton → Manchester United	£33.3
Luke Shaw	18	Southampton → Manchester United	£33.75
Vinícius Júnior	18	Flamengo → Real Madrid	£40.5
Rodrygo	17	Santos FC → Real Madrid	£40.5
Kylian Mbappé	18	AS Monaco → Paris Saint-Germain	Loan (£166)

Source: Transfermarkt (correct as of January 2019)

Summary

- The most crucial point regarding youth rules is to always err on the side of caution – the first port of call when trying to find the necessary regulations should be the relevant association's website, and contacting a representative is strongly advised.

- The punishment for not following the rules correctly can be extremely serious – breaking the law, especially when concerning minors, must be avoided.
- Although the FFF explicitly calls for a legal representative to oversee the Representation Contract between an agent and a minor, it is advised to seek legal consultation in whatever country you are located in to make sure no rules are being breached.

The expert's view: David Jackett (Global football consultant and agent)

Youth football is its own sphere, network and world. The modern game views young players as both low-risk commodities and high-quantity 'investments' with the potential of great reward for the successful few.

A magnifying glass has been focused on youth football like never before, due to amplified worldwide passion from fans. This is coupled with an increased ability for a supporter to follow updates on a player from the other side of the planet. The demand for content overspills into 'Who is the next young, home-grown star of the team?' This globalised modern world brands young footballers as prospects, ensuring a 'bandwagon' surrounding the next big star from all angles. Millennials have now subconsciously bought into the 'rising star' philosophy through social media. This creates a very different perception to the apprentice reality of today, with old academies being challenged to adapt their teachings in increasingly lucrative and consequently deceptive surroundings. It is this evolution which will not lead to more players earning a living, but will bring out the best in existing domestic talent who, from the age of twelve, face international competition with more basic upbringings at elite clubs.

The underbelly of the beautiful game raises questions about each child's journey by writers, coaches, parents and players. Roles are blurred. Injuries occur. There are social pressures. Passion overspills. A normal childhood can be sacrificed, but the opportunities that come with the prize of success are often far too good to turn down.

CHAPTER SIX

WORKING WITH MANAGERS AND SPORTING DIRECTORS

Although this book centres around the player–agent relationship, the representation of other individuals within the sport is becoming increasingly pertinent and important. More and more top managers and sporting directors are receiving professional advice from intermediaries, with specific agencies being set up to offer exactly this. For example, Project B (the company that represents manager Jürgen Klopp, amongst others) showcases this new and developing type of agency as they focus not on players but those in management positions. Whilst the skills required to represent such clients are similar, there are some important differences to note.

Being the agent of a manager

Much like football players, managers need professional representation. Even though they are less likely to bring you lucrative sponsorship deals, there are still opportunities to be successful through the contracts they sign with clubs. Whereas with football players there are strict rules and regulations on representing them, there are no such fixed guidelines or practices that have to be adhered to with managers. However, despite there being no fixed limit on commission, it is generally assumed that the agent is entitled to around 10% as a reward for their work in negotiating the contract.

Manager	Club	Salary
Diego Simeone	Atlético Madrid	€41.00m
José Mourinho	Manchester United (ex)	€31.00m
Thierry Henry	AS Monaco (ex)	€25.50m
Pep Guardiola	Manchester City	€24.00m
Ernesto Valverde	Barcelona	€20.50m
Arsène Wenger	Arsenal (ex)	€15.00m
Fabio Cannavaro	Guangzhou Evergrande	€13.50m
Massimiliano Allegri	Juventus	€13.00m
Jürgen Klopp	Liverpool	€13.00m
Marcello Lippi	China (ex)	€13.00m

Source: Transfermarkt (correct as of April 2019)

Advantages of representing a manager

In addition to the negotiated commission, there are numerous benefits to being the agent of a football manager. If you represent the manager, it gives you the opportunity to utilise this important figure at the club in order to make transfers for others among your clients. This practice is frequently employed by lots of agents. For example, Jorge Mendes has acted as the registered intermediary for both player and manager in many transfer negotiations. The following table details some of these deals as all the listed players are represented by Mendes and were transferred to a club where the manager is also a client of his (José Mourinho in these examples).

By working in this way, you will always have a link to the club where the manager is at, even when they leave. Furthermore, the manager you represent can easily introduce you to other key employees at the club, which can strengthen your position if you already manage a player there. For example, if through the manager you improve your relations with other important decision-makers, it is more likely that your player will be treated favourably, perhaps in terms of being picked for the team, or when discussing a new contract.

Player	Year	Transfer	Fee
Paulo Ferreira	2004–05	Porto → Chelsea	£18m
Tiago	2004–05	Benfica → Chelsea	£13.5m

Ricardo Carvalho	2004–05	Porto → Chelsea	£27m
Nuno Morais	2004–05	Penafiel → Chelsea	Free
Ricardo Quaresma	2008–09	Porto → Inter Milan	£22.1m
Ángel Di María	2010–11	Benfica → Real Madrid	£29.7m
Ricardo Carvalho	2010–11	Chelsea → Real Madrid	£7.2m
Fábio Coentrão	2011–12	Benfica → Real Madrid	£27m
Diego Costa	2014–15	Atlético Madrid → Chelsea	£34.2m

Source: Transfermarkt *(correct as of January 2019)*

Young managers

In modern football, young managers are increasingly used by top clubs around the world, and therefore it is important to try and establish good connections with these promising coaches. Usually, young managers will start their career by taking charge of the lower youth teams (U17 or U19), and slowly work their way up to the U23 team or second team. It is often the case that, when the manager of the main team is sacked or resigns, the board look to these coaches, who understand the set-up of the club so well, in order to assume responsibility for the first team. The same logic can be easily applied to the existing assistant manager, who can also temporarily (and then permanently) fill the vacant managerial spot. Consequently, it is beneficial to have good relationships with young and promising managers, as frequently they will become the first-team manager in years to come.

Working alongside a sporting director

The key advice to remember when working with a sporting director (or any club official besides the manager) is to try and get into their mind and way of thinking, and this is where your understanding of football – as well as keeping up to date with all news and transfers – is crucial. Using all the resources that you have, you have to try and predict what the sporting director needs for their club in terms of players. If, for example, the team has sold its starting striker or their striker gets injured, it could be clever for you to get a mandate for a striker's transfer and try to sell them to that club.

Additionally, there is another way in which an agent can work with a sporting director or a senior club official. Whilst getting a mandate for a player's transfer is common, getting a mandate from the club to conduct its transfer policy is happening more frequently. The club authorises you to contact potential players on their behalf, whilst you receive an agreed commission for your services. Such agreements between an agent and sporting director are often kept secret so that the club doesn't have to bind itself to the recommendations of a single intermediary.

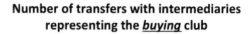

**Number of transfers with intermediaries
representing the _buying_ club**

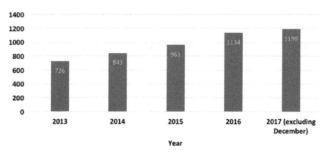

Source: FIFA TMS – Intermediaries in International Transfer (2017 edition)

Summary

- Although it may not seem as rewarding as being the agent of a high-profile player, representing senior club officials can be greatly advantageous as they often open doors and allow you access to the team's transfer dealings.
- Many agents (and agencies) opt for a mix between players and club executives in order to get the benefits of being close to both types of client.
- You must always be aware of the intentions of managers and officials – they are likely to have 'closed-door' relationships with many intermediaries in the hope of getting the best possible deals for themselves.

The expert's view: Harun Arslan
(Owner, ARP Sportmarketing GmbH)

At first glance you may think that there aren't really any significant differences between representing a player and representing a club employee (such as a manager, coach or director). After all, you treat both as important clients, and both entail work such as contractual matters and monetary terms. Whilst this is correct, there are some key distinctions that should be made.

Firstly, you have to take into consideration the age of the client. For a player (especially if they are young), the agent often takes up the role of an additional parent, whereas with a coach you ought to expect a completely different dynamic. Coaches are generally experienced personalities, and top-level managers work in a highly complex environment. A coach is expected to always stay focused, and every single word or action reflects on the club they are contracted to. Although it is in the interests of the club to protect its employees, the relationship with an agent has a special function. You act with the necessary distance to give neutral advice in all circumstances and provide clarity in difficult situations, making tough decisions easier. In many ways, the agent of a club employee is like a good friend – you are there to provide unbiased support with the best intentions.

In addition to making sure your client presents a 'good image' to the public, working in this area of football will involve you in important contractual and career decisions, as well as establishing a strong network to be utilised in the future. In the current game, on-pitch failure usually leads to the dismissal of coaches, managers and other club employees, thus making your job exceedingly important.

CHAPTER SEVEN

THE ART OF A TRANSFER

As discussed in the previous chapter, one of the key components of the football world is transfers. The most common type is the permanent transfer, which occurs when the purchasing club technically buys the player out of their contract – this is therefore akin to a form of compensation. The important question for the purpose of this book is where the agent fits into an agreement that is technically made between two clubs. The key to answering this question lies in the technical term for agents: 'intermediaries'. By acting as the mediator between the two teams, you are a crucial piece of the transfer puzzle, as often, without agents, deals cannot be brokered.

Preparation for the window

Football agents often joke that the transfer window has no start and no end. Although the dates provided give you the actual days on which transfers can be finalised, the work that goes into them starts long before the deal takes place. It is rare that any deal (even if it is completed towards the end of the window) hasn't been the subject of talks between the agent of the player and representatives of the club for weeks, if not months. Therefore, it is crucial for you to be constantly monitoring the needs of clubs in case a player you represent (or have a mandate for) fits the requirements as you see them. This research could be as easy as looking up when key players are 'out of contract', or simply knowing what teams are lacking position-wise. Transfer windows can often be the pinnacle of the work you have been putting in all year round – but remember, do not rush or be forced into any deal, and always keep in close contact with clients in order to know what they want.

Country	Pre-season window	Mid-season window	Record transfer (£ M; €/$ M)
England (FA)	17th May – 9th August	1st January – 31st January	Paul Pogba (£89, €105)
Germany (DFB)	1st July – 31st August	1st January – 2nd February	Corentin Tolisso (£38, €41.5)
France (FFF)	9th June – 31st August	1st January – 31st January	Neymar Jr. (£200, €222)

Spain (RFEF)	1st July – 1st September	1st January – 2nd February	Philippe Coutinho (£108, €120)
Italy (FIGC)	1st July – 18th August	3rd January – 31st January	Cristiano Ronaldo (£88, €100)
Portugal (FPF)	7th July – 21st September	3rd January – 2nd February	Raúl Jiménez (£20, €22)
Neth-erlands (KNVB)	11th June – 2nd September	3rd January – 31st January	Daley Blind (£14 , €17)
United States of America (USSF)	7th February – 1st May	10th July – 8th August	Gonzalo Martínez (£12, ~$10)
Turkey (TFF)	11th June– 1st September	5th January– 31st January	Jardel (£15, €17)
Australia (FFA)	24th July – 15th October	3rd January – 31st January	Shane Smeltz (£0.8, $1.2)

Source: Transfermarkt (correct as of January 2019)

The strategy of the agent

As already mentioned, the situation your client finds themselves in is what usually dictates your work with regards to transfers. This can be split into three different categories:

1. *Your client wants to leave.* The reasons for this can vary from falling out with the coach to not receiving enough playing time, to simply wanting a new challenge. It then becomes your duty to find a new club that fits in with what the player wants. Of course, it is rare to find a team that matches your client's expectations perfectly

in terms of location, league position etc, and who are also in a financial position to make a move – but this is where you show your worth!

2. **Your client's team wants to sell.** This results in a very similar situation to the above scenario, as you'll again be looking for a new club for your client. However, in this type of situation, it is easy to neglect and alienate your player's current club – you should not take its decision to sell your client personally. Remember, football is a business, and players are still technically under the contract of their club.

3. **Another club wants to buy your client.** You should always present your player with the offers that are proposed for them, as they have a right to know. A reasonable question to ask here is how the agent knows about what offers come in for client if a transfer agreement is conducted between clubs. Essentially, buying clubs are aware of the crucial role and the decision-making power of the agent. Therefore, they usually contact the intermediary first as they know the deal cannot happen without them.

Role of the agent in a transfer agreement

Simply put, agents are pivotal to the transfer process. By being the middleman between the two clubs, you *can* essentially be acting on behalf of all parties. Once a consensus has been reached by the buying and selling clubs over the exchange of the player, your role is to try and make sure that the deal happens. Perhaps the most common stumbling point for a deal is the fee. You have to try and help structure the deal so it looks like both sides are winning and benefiting from the agreement. This is where negotiation skills and being able to read the situation well are key. You must try to understand and work out what the buying club sees as a reasonable figure, and what the selling club would accept as a bottom line. More often than not, an individual transfer is part of a much wider set of deals that are taking place. If a club is losing one of their top strikers because they want to leave, then it is likely that the club will have targets in mind to replace them. Consequently, they want to ensure that any possible incomings are probable before committing to a sale.

In general, all transfers are different – scenarios vary from league to league and club to club – so much of the process is about being able to adapt to situations quickly. There will be times when the deal looks almost certain to have fallen through, but the smallest event could re-energise talks, and you have to be ready for this at all times.

Spending on club intermediary commissions from January 2013 to November 2017 (US$ million)

Country	Buying club	Selling club	Total
England	433.4	56.5	489.9
Italy	257.8	86.0	343.8
Portugal	74.6	86.6	161.2

Germany	119.0	26.7	145.7
Spain	99.0	22.7	121.7
France	35.3	26.2	61.5
Belgium	8.3	23.1	31.4
Russia	22.5	8.2	30.7
Wales	25.7	3.6	29.3
Croatia	5.6	14.3	19.9

Source: FIFA TMS — Intermediaries in International Transfer (2017 edition)

Mandates

Everything discussed thus far is in relation to you as the agent in transfer negotiations with a client you represent (as signified by a Representation Contract – see Chapter 9). However, you can even be involved in transfers for players that you don't work with every day, or don't even know! Either you can get a mandate from another player/ agent, or from a club.

1. *Mandate from another player/agent.* Depending on what exactly was agreed, a mandate means that you would handle just the player's transfer for a certain period of time (normally one transfer window) to a certain league or country. This is beneficial for both you and the full-time agent of the player. Firstly, it gives you an opportunity to make a deal happen that you

wouldn't otherwise have had, whilst not having the workload of looking after the player fully. It is also advantageous for the player and their agent because they may not have the network or connections to clubs to make a transfer possible – therefore mandates mean the deal can still occur without them necessarily being at the forefront of negotiations. In these deals, the commission is normally split as specified in the mandate agreement itself.

2. *Mandate from a club.* Whilst these types of arrangements are rarely disclosed to the public, clubs have certain agents they like to go back to in order to make deals happen. Essentially, the club gives you a mandate for either a player or a region/league, and your commission would be paid for by the club. However, with most top teams having a position akin to a director of football, they usually handle transfers instead of a mandated intermediary and therefore could cut you out as the mediator. This is why it is important you try to get everything in writing, and keep on good terms with all involved.

Overall, mandates are certainly a worthwhile consideration for an agent. An up-and-coming agent and player may agree on a mandate for a transfer as a trial period for future representation, as it is sometimes thought of as a test of the ability of an agent.

Transfer fee

When reading about transfers in the news or on social media, it may be reported that a footballer leaves a club, for example, for a fee of £100 million. Of course, that's a substantial sum of money, and, despite how it is reported, transfers aren't as simple as one club sending over a lump sum in exchange for a signature. The fact these newspaper reports do not consider performance-based add-ons, instalments and wage packages renders them inaccurate, and it is important to know how transfer fees are structured.

- *Add-ons.* If Player X moves from Club Y to Club Z for an agreed £100 million, then the entirety of that fee may not be guaranteed. A reasonable percentage may be subject to the performance of the player (e.g. number of appearances, goals, personal accolades etc.) or the performance of the club (promotion, relegation, league position etc.), meaning the final fee can vary significantly.
- *Instalments.* Nearly all transfer fees are exchanged over an extended period of time. Using the same transfer structure as above, then perhaps only 50% of the £100 million is paid upon completion. On the first anniversary of the deal, another 25% may be transferred, and the same again on the second anniversary.
- *Wages.* If a club is willing to pay a vast sum like £100 million, then clearly it is an elite player in question. Newspaper reports rarely refer to the wages the players will earn as part of the overall package that

Club Z (the buying club) will pay. If Player X is to receive a weekly wage of £150,000 on a four-year contract, then this is an additional £31.2 million that Club Z is spending. This adds on essentially another third of the transfer fee, making for a total investment of £131.2 million.

From this it is clear that more goes into a transfer negotiation than is first envisaged. Not included in this pay structure is what you would earn as the agent. Although the Representation Contract is between player and agent, it is nearly always the case that the club ends up paying the agent their commission fee. Although many agents (immorally) go to clubs asking which will pay the highest agency fee, the best agents negotiate the greatest deal possible for their client first, and then work out commission. This goes back to a key characteristic of a good agent: you are representing the player first and foremost, acting in their best interests at all times.

The personal side of a transfer

If one considers football to be like any other profession, then transferring clubs (like switching jobs) often entails moving to another city or even country. If this is the case, then multiple things need to be taken into consideration, especially if the player has to go abroad. Will your client have to learn a new language? Should they buy or rent a new house? Will their family come with them? Do they need a work permit? Do they need a new car?

All these questions (and many, many more) are totally valid. Changing teams (even if they don't end up moving to a new country) is still an important and often challenging phase in any player's life. This is where having a good relationship with your player and their club is crucial. The overwhelming majority of top clubs will have people in place to help out incoming players who are new to the area. They will help settle them into the region, teach them a new language if necessary, and make sure they are looked after and feel as comfortable as possible. Additionally, this is where you need to step in. It is also your duty to safeguard your client and guarantee their well-being and comfort. Making sure you yourself speak the language of the country that your client is playing in is very important, and broadening your horizons by speaking multiple languages is another fundamental characteristic of the agency world.

Similarly, given your duty to help your player, it is also important to ensure their family's needs are looked after. Depending on what relationships your client has, relatives may choose to move with them to help settle them in. This can be beneficial to you as it is another layer of comfort for your client.

Winter transfer window: a 2018 case study

In statistics published by FIFA TMS, a close analysis of the winter transfer window of 2018 can be made from the perspective of the 'Big 5' (England, Spain, Germany, France and Italy). According to FIFA, despite the number of total transfers between these associations decreasing by 1.1% in the same period in the year prior, 2018 witnessed over a 70% increase in spending.

Nevertheless, there is a tendency for the big spending to take place in the summer, and FIFA puts this down to clubs preferring to make larger investments at the end of the season. The TMS indicates that between 2011 and 2017, there were seventeen transfers over $30 million to the Big 5 in the winter windows, whereas 112 of these types of deals took place in the summer transfer period.

So, the question to be asked is what allowed for this unprecedented spike in money being exchanged in the winter of 2018? The answer to this lies in the fact that a small handful of huge deals skewed the numbers significantly, with Philippe Coutinho (Liverpool to Barcelona), Virgil van Dijk (Southampton to Liverpool) and Pierre-Emerick Aubameyang (Borussia Dortmund to Arsenal) all large contributors to this.

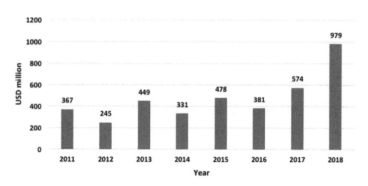

Transfer spending amongst the 'Big 5' during winter transfer windows

Country	Incoming transfers	Outgoing transfers	Spending ($ M)	Receipts ($ M)
England (FA)	141	169	482.8	334.5
Germany (DFB)	86	75	68.3	107.1
France (FFF)	75	75	43.9	90.3
Spain (RFEF)	158	85	361.3	94.4
Italy (FIGC)	70	71	22.8	90.0

Incoming Transfers By Type – England

Incoming Transfers By Type – Germany

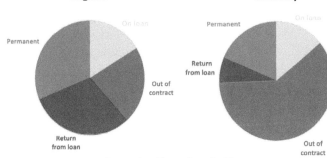

Incoming Transfers By Type – France

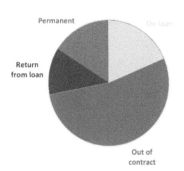

Incoming Transfers By Type – Spain

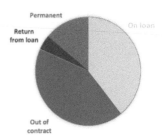

Incoming Transfers By Type – Italy

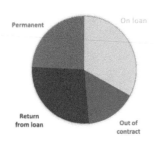

Source: FIFA TMS – Big 5 Transfer Window Analysis, Winter 2018

Summary

- Transfers as a whole are not the straightforward process that is often reported – the complexities of coming to a transfer agreement for a player are not to be underestimated.
- You have to be smart, shrewd and professional at all times with dealing with a transfer – if you have to, use your network to access other trustworthy agents or lawyers to help you.
- Remember, the best agents will see out a transfer from beginning to end – making sure that all parties can benefit, and maintaining the best of relationships even with the club that their player has departed from.

The expert's view: Dr Erkut Sögüt
(Agent of Mesut Özil, Family & Football)

So much time and effort go into a transfer that it is difficult to summarise in a few words. In addition, transfers vary so much by club, by player and by agent, meaning that no two deals are really the same. In my experience, it's rare that a transfer is straightforward. When you're dealing with humans and large amounts of money, then complications always arise.

That's why preparation is key. Make sure you have the necessary documentation and authority at all times. If you know a club wants a striker, don't go telling them that you represent a potential player whom you've only met once or twice. This makes you look unprofessional and can undermine your credibility. Instead, get a mandate for the deal, or speak with the player and/or their representatives. Remember, things in the football business can move quickly (especially towards the end of a transfer window), so make sure you're ready for action.

As an agent, it's inevitable that you will be part of deals that nearly happen but don't quite get over the line. Especially when first starting out, this is frustrating. You put all the right work in but for whatever reason beyond your control, that deal doesn't go through. I know it's tough and demoralising, but this is the industry that we're in! It doesn't make you a bad agent; it makes you a more motivated agent, and the eventual deal you negotiate even sweeter. This is the mentality you need to have. Don't get down and give up. Keep going, work harder, work smarter and you'll realise that patience is a virtue!

CHAPTER EIGHT

LOANS AND 'FREE AGENTS'

Whilst permanent transfers were covered in the previous chapter, two other common types of deal have yet to be properly addressed: loans and 'free agents'. Agents require knowledge of both of these if they are to succeed in the industry. Whilst headlines are often dominated by news of permanent deals, the following table illustrates the frequency of these two alternative methods of transfer.

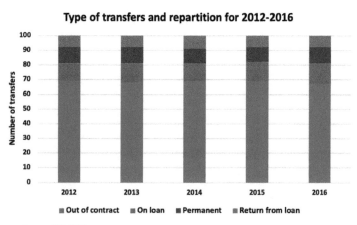

Type of transfers and repartition for 2012-2016

Source: FIFA TMS

What is a loan?

A loan is the temporary transfer of a player from one club to another. Such deals are so popular that some clubs (like Chelsea) have their own loan department where people are employed just to look after the loaned players and visit them during the season in order to check their development. A loan can vary in length and depends on what the two clubs agree on; however, they are normally for the duration of the season (or for the second half of a season). It is very common for the 'parent club' to ask for either a contribution to the wages of the player or a sum of money for the duration of the loan. Both of these scenarios require you as the agent to be active in the negotiations. Lots of teams have a 'feeder club' in another country in which they loan younger or unused players to. Well-known examples of this include Chelsea's relationship with Vitesse, and Manchester City's relationship with other members of the City Football Group.

Advantages of loans

From the perspective of a player and their agent, loans can be of great use and benefit:

1. *Playing time.* If your client is given more playing time at another club, it could showcase their potential worth for the parent club in the future, or increase their transfer value if you are looking for a permanent move elsewhere.

2. *International fixture lists.* Using the USA's MLS (Major League Soccer) as an example, the season starts at a completely different time to that of European leagues, and therefore players can be loaned from the USA to Europe during their 'off-season'. A well-known example of this is Landon Donovan, who, whilst at the LA Galaxy, was loaned to Bayern Munich and Everton whilst the MLS was inactive. This was beneficial for both LA Galaxy, as it meant he stayed in shape, and Bayern Munich and Everton, as he was a good on-pitch option to have. Moreover, for the player (and thus agent), it meant that Donovan became more of a household name across Europe, increasing not only his footballing value and experience but in addition the scope for commercial deals given his greater global notability.

Options to buy

The supposed middle ground between a loan and permanent deal is often deemed to be the 'option to buy clause'. This involves a club agreeing to loan a player for a certain amount of time, with an agreement also being in place for a full transfer. This strategy is becoming more common for clubs as they can test the player out, without having the obligation of a permanent deal. Recent examples of this can be found with top European players, such as James Rodríguez (Real Madrid and Bayern Munich) and Douglas Costa (Bayern Munich and Juventus). Sometimes whether or not the full transfer takes place is down to appearance- and performance-based clauses that were initially agreed – these will have been made clear, and it is for you as the agent to be involved in the deal-making process. This method of transfer has also been adapted in recent transfer windows. The agreement between Monaco and Paris Saint-Germain regarding Kylian Mbappé has been labelled as an 'obligation to buy' rather than an 'option to buy', with the latter club supposedly required to follow through with the deal after the loan period has come to an end. Either way, an agent must be aware of the possible uses of both methods.

What is a 'free agent'?

When a player is about to be out of contract, they are deemed to be a 'free agent'. This is because they are able to sign with any club they want to, with no transfer fee having to be paid. This method of transfer originated from the landmark court case in 1995, resulting in the 'Bosman ruling'. This meant that players could move to a new club without their previous team receiving a fee. Players could now sign a 'pre-contract' with another team if their contract had less than six months remaining. For agents with clients playing in the English league, do note there is a rule that you aren't technically allowed to start having discussions with other English teams before the final six months of the contract.

Benefits and risks of 'free agency'

The advantages to representing a free agent tend to be about money and freedom of choice:

1. **Money.** Given that clubs do not have to pay any transfer fee, there is far more scope to negotiate a bigger salary for your client. Some of the largest wages known to date are those of players who moved as a free agent or a renegotiation that took place in the final six months of the Employment Contract, when there is the possibility that the club could lose the player for free. Whilst many criticise players moving for monetary reasons, ultimately it is your job to represent the player's wishes – and 'free agency' can often offer life-changing amounts.

2. **Freedom of choice.** Another fantastic benefit of 'free agency' is in essence the player has the power to pick what club they want to go to. Because there is no negotiation between the two clubs, you can go directly to teams (and teams can also go directly to you). If your player has always dreamed of playing for a certain club, or in a particular country, then being a free agent tends to be a fantastic opportunity.

Whilst the aforementioned advantages are clearly apparent, they do not come without some risks and downsides:

1. **Injury.** If your client suffers a serious injury towards the end of their contract, then this will be detrimental in

finding a new club. Despite them not being a big risk for a prospective club given the lack of transfer fee, there is no real need for a team to sign an injured player (who they will have to cover medical bills for) until they are fit and fully recovered. Therefore, if your client suffers a significant injury and doesn't have a club, it could mean having to deal with rehab and recovery independently.

2. *Time.* The fact that most contracts nowadays are signed on a five-year basis means that waiting for a client to become a free agent is a lengthy process that could detract from making the most out of a player's career. If the initial contract is signed in a player's late twenties, then demanding a substantial pay cheque over the age of thirty is by no means always easy, and it is relatively rare that players actually end up staying at a team long enough to become a free agent.

Summary

- Both loans and 'free agent' deals come with obvious upsides and must always be under consideration as an agent.
- For loan deals, just because the transfer isn't permanent, it doesn't mean that you can be more relaxed or less scrupulous or involved in the decision-making process – you have to be on top of the deal at all times, even if the move is only for a few months.
- Even though 'free agency' can bring big money, you must always advise your player with their best interests

in mind. Don't selfishly advise a client to wait out years of a contract just so they can become a free agent and get a more lucrative deal – always think about the bigger picture, and what is best for them.

The expert's view: Loren Román García (Agent of Lucas Pérez, Family & Football)

In today's game, both of these types of transfer are really important to know about and use when appropriate.

Loans are great because of their versatility in allowing the player to move to another club and increase their worth without actually making any permanent decisions. Whether you're a youth player, a player stuck in the reserves or a player wanting a change of scenery, loans give you this flexibility. With increased rules regulating clubs' spending, many permanent deals also take place in the form of a loan. The majority of 'options to buy' usually develop into full transfers, or at least a transfer to another interested club after the (hopefully positive) loan spell.

The concept of 'free agency' is so interesting for an agent. A player is free to go to any club they want to, and essentially becomes the focus of a bidding war for their services. Whoever can offer the best package normally wins the player. It *can* be such a great position to be in as an agent. But it comes with its risks: injury, and the inability to find a willing club, as well as any unforeseen issues that can crop up.

CHAPTER NINE

CONTRACTS

Perhaps the most complex aspect of being a football agent is dealing with the contracts and negotiations on behalf of your client. Such contracts can be easily separated into two categories: those that are directly related to your player's career and those that deal with the more personal side of their affairs. Even though negotiating stances vary according to the person, there are still certain things that have to be considered when dealing with contracts. Furthermore, it should be noted that taking the advice of a qualified financial advisor or lawyer is a good idea, and is sometimes a requirement.

Representation Contract

In order to legitimately represent a player, there has to be a valid Representation Contract between you and your client, as well as, of course, you being registered as an intermediary (see Chapter 2 for details). This agreement, which is valid for two years, is an extremely important part of the process. The Representation Contract is normally agreed alongside the agent's fee (a certain percentage of the player's salary as agreed by the Employment Contract), and includes a portion of the signing-on fee whilst usually excluding other bonuses like goals or appearances. The recognised norm that an agent receives is up to 10% of a client's gross salary per year, but this varies greatly depending on the club, player and agent. Interestingly, the Dutch (KNVB) regulations state that, if agent and club fail to come to an agreement about the commission rate, then 3% of the gross annual salary is awarded to the agent.

It is important to note that, if the Employment Contract is due to end after the Representation Contract, the intermediary is still entitled to their agreed percentage.

Despite being a relatively straightforward contract, there are some basic things that agents often get wrong. The most common of these is to do with the names provided. Even if you work for an agency, you should **always** put your name, and not the name of the agency. This is simply because, if you were to leave that firm, you would have difficulties taking your client with you given that the agency (and not you) would technically represent them per the Representation Contract. Also, despite this sounding obvious, do make sure both your name and that of your client are spelt correctly!

In England (FA), the Representation Contract has two years before it needs to be renewed. However, a common question posed is what if the player wants to leave their agent before the contract expires? Looking at this from the agent's perspective, there are some key things to consider:

1. Firstly, if you're doing a good job, then this shouldn't happen! But of course, scenarios like these do occur, and you must remain professional at all times.
2. When you initially agree the Representation Contract, try to ensure it is done on the basis of exclusivity. Whilst this issue is contentious in countries like Germany (which, by law, bans exclusive representation, although many German agents do it anyway), this is not a law in other countries.
3. Using the example of England, where the Representation Contract is two years long, you don't have to wait until it is about to expire before renewing it. If you manage to get your client a transfer, new contract, or something else of benefit, then it could be a good time to ask them if they are willing to renew the Representation Contract.
4. If after all attempts your client still wants to leave you, try to make sure the next agent they sign with is someone who you can cooperate with and potentially share commission with on future deals.

Transfers with intermediaries representing the player from January 2013 to November 2017

Player nationality	Transfers	As a % of all transfers
Danish	234	43.7%
Dutch	441	38.1%
American	332	36.4%
Canadian	87	36.0%
Israeli	77	35.5%
Australian	163	33.2%
Austrian	148	33.0%
Czech	174	32.5%
Jamaican	65	30.4%
German	279	30.2%

Source: FIFA TMS – Intermediaries in International Transfer (2017 edition)

Employment Contract

The contractual relationship between a player and a club is encapsulated in the Employment Contract. This is something that is agreed when the player joins a club (after a transfer). The Employment Contract would normally cover a series of different aspects between the two parties – for example, it may include a signing-on bonus as well as appearance or goal bonuses. Here, it would be for the agent of the player to negotiate on their client's behalf, in order to secure the best possible deal. It is very common for much of a player's income to actually come from these bonuses and not only from their standard wage. For contracts with Premier League players, personal terms are set out in Schedule 2 of the standard contract – so everything from the basic wage to bonuses to compensation is agreed in this part. Under the Representation Contract (explained before), the agent of a player is entitled to their commission and this is closely linked with the Employment Contract. Often, it is thought that players are the ones who pay their agent, but it is the club that does this, as clubs pay the agent the negotiated percentage on top of the wages they pay the player. As always, it is crucial for the intermediary to be aware of the rules set out by FIFA and the relevant footballing association regarding contracts, making sure that all the criteria have been followed and adhered to.

Contract renewals

When you read about players 'renewing' or signing a 'new contract', this refers to the Employment Contract. Contract renewals can occur at any point before the expiration of the initial contract, and can be the result of numerous scenarios:

1. *There is interest in your client from another club.* If your player is the subject of an enquiry or bid from another team that is rejected, then this provides a great opportunity for a renegotiation of the Employment Contract. Clearly, your client is in demand and another club felt that their value exceeded their current contract. Therefore, this provides you with a perfectly logical opportunity for a renewal.

2. ***Towards the end of the current Employment Contract.*** As detailed in the previous chapter, some of the biggest contracts to exist have come off the back of 'free agency'. Given how the threat of becoming a 'free agent' can be a frightening prospect for the player's current club, as they risk losing their asset for free, players approaching 'free agency' hold an equally powerful position. These scenarios can result in just as lucrative contract renegotiations despite the player staying put.

3. ***A breakout season.*** If your client has greatly exceeded all expectations and is playing at a level that clearly surpasses their current contract, then this is an obvious opening for you. This often occurs when a young talent is given a first-team role and delivers some great performances.

4. ***Teammates.*** If your player's club makes a move in the transfer window and signs a player to a much higher wage, or renegotiates a current teammate's salary, then there *may* be scope for you to have some discussions regarding your client. If you can reasonably argue that the difference in pay is far greater than the difference in talent and on-pitch (and also off-pitch commercial) value, then there could be grounds for a renewal.

Tripartite Representation Contract

In most cases, an agent represents the club (for the purposes of the transfer) and the player at the same time, thus leading to an obvious conflict of interests. However, given the inevitability of this conflict, this dual representation is permitted by the footballing associations (again, check the rules for the relevant federation). In order for the agent to be allowed to act on behalf of both parties, they must abide by all the regulations and submit the applicable paperwork. Using the example of England (FA), the agent must also sign off on the Tripartite Representation Contract, a document that confirms the process of dual representation. In the case of the Netherlands (KNVB), dual representation is allowed, but only after the club has granted written permission.

Summary

- Given the legal importance of contracts, it is always advisable to have a strong relationship with a lawyer (or law firm) you can trust to give you impartial guidance and help.
- As the agent, you will play an integral role in every negotiation and agreement that is made with regards to your client – it is therefore crucial that you check over every detail and leave nothing to chance.
- Furthermore, you should always keep your client well informed about every decision that you plan on making, as it is on their behalf that you are negotiating.

The expert's view: Daniel Geey (Sports lawyer, Sheridans)

For high-profile, elite footballers, there are a number of considerations when signing important football-related contracts. A robust Representation Contract which sets out the relationship between player and agent is vital. The Representation Contract will include the following elements which agents and players need to understand:

- The contract is for the **maximum two years** possible under the rules, to ensure that players are not tied to an agent for too long.
- The contract is **exclusive** (as far as legally possible in particular countries), so that, during the length of the contract, no other agent can represent the player. If another agent claims to represent the player, and the first agent is then cut out of the deal and loses out on commission, it is likely that the player can be sued for breach of contract by their original agent.
- The agent has the power to represent the player when negotiating transfers, Employment Contracts and commercial deals. It is important for the agent that they can earn commission not just from on-field transfer and contract renegotiations, but also from all commercial agreements (including, for example, an Adidas boot deal). This enables the agent on behalf of the player to **maximise earnings on and off the pitch**.
- The **commission rate** for negotiating a player's new contract or transfer can be between 3% and 10% of the player's total salary. However, when negotiating commercial deals (a boot deal, say, or a skincare deal), agents are usually entitled to receive between 15% and 20% of the value of the endorsement agreement.

CHAPTER TEN

SOCIAL MEDIA AND MARKETING

With the game of football no longer being confined to the pitch, as an agent you have to be constantly thinking about how to make the most of the platform your client has. Remember, sport is one of the few industries in which workers (i.e. the athletes) have a relatively short window of opportunity. Given that the on-pitch career of a footballer is normally no longer than fifteen years, you have to make sure that commercial and marketing deals (as well as investments – see Chapter 12) are done whilst the player is still active and has an engaged global reach. Although the stereotype of a lavish lifestyle is not applicable to every player, additional off-pitch agreements can provide financial stability post career. This idea is particularly relevant to long-term investments, as they give your client a constant source of income when they are no longer receiving lucrative playing contracts. The role of the agent in all this is of paramount importance. You'll typically be the one making these deals and ventures happen, and, unlike the commission cap of an Employment Contract, these types of arrangements have no maximum commission limit, although the norm is 15–20%.

Image Rights Agreement

A crucial element of the contract negotiations between the player (via the agent) and the club is the Image Rights Agreement. If your client is well known (or has the potential to be a household name), then this part of the contract becomes even more significant. The Image Rights Agreement ensures that the player receives a percentage of the money the club gains after using their image commercially. Consequently, it would be for the agent to help form a company that would specifically be used to give permission for the rights to the player's image. In some cases, the club will have sold its own image rights to a third-party company. Consequently, if a player from this team were to sign a sponsorship agreement, it would be wise (as their agent) to negotiate a deal based on material gifts (and a small fee) rather than a larger cash sum. Such an agreement is labelled 'value in kind' (VIK). Doing this would ensure that both you and your client receive the utmost from the situation.

Under the Image Rights Agreement, much of the commercial activity of a footballer is already dictated and somewhat restricted. This is because no player can enter into a sponsorship agreement with a company that is a competitor of a primary/principal sponsor of the club. For example, if your client played for Manchester City, which has Etihad Airways as a principal sponsor, then you could not go about seeking a commercial agreement with an airline competitor. A list of sponsors (and by implication industries with which your player can't have an endorsement deal) can be found on the club's website and is typically stated in the Employment Contract/Image Rights Agreement itself too. If you think you may be entering a deal that would come into conflict with the club, then get legal advice and speak with a trustworthy contact at the club.

Boot deals

Having just stated that it is not permitted to have a sponsorship deal with a competitor of a primary sponsor of your player's club, there is **one** exception to this rule: boot deals. Nearly all professional footballers will have some sort of agreement with a sports apparel company, and more influential players will be featured in campaigns and photoshoots. Here, it is up to you as the agent to coordinate these media days (an exact number is negotiated and stated in the marketing contract), making sure they take place after training and when your client has no prior engagements.

But before any of this, the sports brand that you choose (alongside your player) has to be a cautious decision, making sure you weigh up the pros and cons of each company. Whilst having an extremely large sponsor like Nike is an attractive prospect as they have the resources to offer a larger contract initially, the chances of becoming a 'cover athlete' for such a big brand are far less than perhaps with a company like Under Armour or New Balance, which have a growing football roster. Furthermore, there can certainly be an advantage to having the same apparel sponsor as the club the player is signed to. With a common sponsor, there is an increased impetus for both the club and company to include the player in advertising campaigns due to the brand coordination. This obviously brings about a relatively easy commercial opportunity that is well remunerated through the Image Rights Agreement. These have to be careful considerations for not only established professionals but youth players too. With younger athletes, big sports brands will normally send out their own network of scouts to try and discover the best talent before they are in a position to demand a large deal. Either way, ensure that you remain open with your client about which apparel company is possible as they may have their own idea about who they want, and of course this has to be considered too. Remember, the best boot deal isn't **just** the one that pays the most; it's also the one that gives your client the most opportunities going forward in the long run (in terms of exposure and money) and the one your player feels the most comfortable representing.

Endorsement deals

As already alluded to, boot deals are the most common type of sponsorship deal that a footballer can have, and are easier than other areas of endorsement because they are exempt from the primary sponsor rule. However, top agents will be working hard to try and get their clients extra sources of income through paid partnerships and deals that go beyond boots and apparel. In general, there are four key considerations before making any commercial agreement:

1. **Type of brand.** Does this company fit your client's personality and values? Does it come into conflict with a principal sponsor of their club? If the company doesn't reflect what your player feels is important or is interested in, then perhaps it isn't the right partner. Similarly, being endorsed by a business that goes against religious or cultural beliefs could obviously be detrimental. Remember, whatever the public's opinion of this brand may be, it is now inescapably linked to your client – be that for good or bad.

2. **Territory.** Is the deal regional or global? Many large companies have region-specific offshoots. Therefore, is the endorsement for the brand global, or confined to a certain country or continent? This is a very important differentiation – global partnerships will normally mean more money, but regional deals are normally less risky as they can be less encompassing and **may** allow your client to enter into agreements with companies in (relatively) similar areas.

3. **Requirements.** Part of the negotiation process will be to agree on what is actually required from the player. Social media posts, photoshoots, live appearances, and interviews can all be part of the contract between player and sponsor, so make sure that your client is comfortable with what they have to do.

4. ***Length and value of contract.*** As with any agreement, how long it is and the remuneration are two of the most crucial aspects. Ensure that the length of commitment is adequately represented in what is being paid.

In general, just make sure you are cautious in your decision-making and keep the player updated with key developments. Unless you represent an iconic superstar, the more endorsement deals you have results in each future one being worth less as the brand recognition decreases. This is sometimes why one-off social media posts or promotions (combined with some endorsements) can be a good alternative to having lots of long-term sponsorship deals. Moreover, the types of deals discussed so far are based on a purely monetary arrangement, and actually not all deals are solely financial. For example, an agreement with a car company or watch manufacturer may mainly be paid in free gifts (and a small fee on the side) due to the worth of the item being so high.

You may be thinking that this area of the profession is difficult to get into and having the established network and contact list of appropriate brands doesn't come instantly. Some footballers and agents collectively decide to sell the player's image rights to a media agency for a guaranteed fee plus a split of commission. Below is a list of some media and marketing agencies known for working directly with footballers.

Head office	Agency
Los Angeles	Creative Artists Agency (CAA)
London	MediaCom
Munich	We Play Forward
London	CSM Sport & Entertainment
New York	Roc Nation
London	D2S Media
London	The Goat Agency

Social media

A critical component of the commercialisation of footballers is social media, and it is vital that your client has a well-established social media presence on the key sites. Part of the reason why the players listed in the upcoming table can attract the most valuable marketing deals is because their social media following is so large and can therefore reach the highest amount of potential customers for the brand. It is common either for the agent to control the player's social media, or (perhaps for more famous clients) for them to organise a digital agency to help with the accounts and posts. In both situations, it is important that the messages given to fans are positive (for example, posting a picture of the player working hard at training or in the gym), and also conform to contractual agreements with the club and sponsors. For example, a company may sponsor a player to wear their sportswear, and the contract states that there is to be a minimum of five posts featuring that brand in a month. You should also try to ensure your client has a presence in other countries' social media channels. For example, Weibo (China) has twice as many users as Twitter, so this can be a very valuable tool to have.

Whilst social media is great, it can also be very dangerous if not taken seriously or carefully. You have to make sure that your client avoids discussing injuries or tactics that can help an opponent, or posting any 'sensitive' material that may cause serious offence. Overall, social media is almost a necessity when it comes to the marketing of football players. It allows the public to gain an unparalleled insight into the personalities of their sporting heroes, therefore making those athletes a more attractive prospect for brands. Simply put, the more content and followers a player has on social media, the more of a brand they are able to build around themselves, which will only result in a greater number of commercial opportunities.

Player	Instagram followers (M)	Facebook followers (M)	Twitter followers (M)	Overall (M)
Cristiano Ronaldo	149	123	76	348
Neymar Jr.	108	61	42	211
Lionel Messi	104	90	N/A	194
James Rodríguez	41	33	18	92
Gareth Bale	38	29	18	85
Andrés Iniesta	27	27	24	78
Mesut Özil	19	32	24	75

Sergio Ramos	29	24	16	69
Zlatan Ibrahimović	36	26	6	68
Luis Suarez	31	19	15	65

Sources: Instagram, Facebook and Twitter (correct as of January 2019)

Personal brands

As already mentioned, social media allows players to build their own personal brand. The notion of a personal brand can take multiple forms. At a basic level, it can be something that a player is known for posting on social media, such as a certain emoji or hashtag. For example, Leroy Sané uses #inSané on most of his posts. Having something like this which fans can constantly relate back to your client is very effective, as the player becomes synonymous with a particular word or remark. Not only can this be attractive for sponsors, but it can allow your client to create their own brand. For example, Arsenal and Manchester United players Mesut Özil and Jesse Lingard both have individual lines of clothing in addition to their boot and apparel deals. Using their respective slogans of 'M10' and 'JLINGZ', they now have an additional off-pitch business venture that benefits from the extensive audience that can be reached through social media. This may lead to you needing to get trademarks for the brand. As the agent, you play a pivotal role in all of this, from the development of your client's social media, to the subsequent exploitation of their enhanced following for off-pitch projects, be they endorsements or personal businesses.

Summary

- The marketing of a football player has become almost as important as the on-field work that is required of an agent. With football growing as a sport year on year, so does the number of big companies trying to get involved by using footballers to push their brand.
- Consulting lawyers with regards to the Image Rights Agreement is advised given how important it is – this contract forms the basis of your client's commercial arrangement with their club, and therefore has considerable value.
- Remember, unless you represent an elite superstar talent, you have to be proactive in reaching out to possible sponsors without seeming desperate or undervaluing your client's worth. The same advice applies to transfers and contracts – not every deal is a good deal!

The expert's view: Chris Wheatley (Director, D2S Media)

As the director of a media agency, you may be asking how my work links in with that of agents and footballers. Much as players need full-time representation with regards to transfers and contracts, they also need this same level of representation when it comes to their public image. Whilst their agent is hugely responsible for this too, my role is to essentially help look after the player off the pitch.

Usually, this comes in the form of social media and marketing opportunities. For example, if a player moves to a club in another country, they may not be able to communicate with their new audience and fanbase as well as they would like to. It is therefore up to me to ensure that things such as their social media channels, interviews and all generic press work are conducted in a comfortable way for the client, and serves to improve (and not harm) their image. The experience I gained in my previous job as a journalist certainly taught me how to deal with different personalities and manage relationships with high-profile individuals.

As mentioned, marketing and sponsorship is another crucial part of my job. Seeking these types of deals for players forms a big part of what a digital agency usually does. This normally comes with being proactive, professional and drawing on years of hard work building up a strong network of contacts. In addition to helping arrange these deals, coordinating the logistics and making sure the player fulfils the contractual duties (social media posts, photoshoots etc.) is another aspect of what we do.

CHAPTER ELEVEN

WORKING WITH THE MEDIA

A common term for mainstream media (newspapers and news outlets), the press is another key area which a successful football agent must be aware of and know how to use to their players' (and therefore their own) advantage. Clearly, not everything in the papers is true, yet the power of the media is extraordinary in modern-day society, and its role in football is equally huge. With the rise of social media, the public no longer need to wait until the newspapers are printed the next day to find the scapegoat for their team's loss, or to know who their club plans on signing on deadline day. This is why having trustworthy connections in the press and media is of vital significance. Of course, as an agent it is impossible to totally control what is said about your client, and it is your duty to try and safeguard them from some of the entirely false things that are published about them. Ultimately, from interviews to articles to newspapers and magazines, knowing how to deal with the various types of media is pivotal.

Interviews and media work

Whereas with social media a content-driven audience necessitates players to post frequently, interviews and media work require a more nuanced approach. The story behind your client's rise, from their dream of becoming a footballer to the reality in which they now find themselves, can only be repeated a limited number of times, so accepting every interview request that comes your way isn't the best thing to do. The last thing you want to do is devalue the worth of your player's comments or story. Therefore, it is recommended that the agent chooses perhaps the most well-known newspapers or interviewers in order to attract the biggest audiences. In addition, timing is a crucial factor. If your client finds themselves in a difficult situation, telling them to go straight to the press to defend themselves isn't always the best approach. Let the situation simmer down a little, and then make a decision wisely. Similarly, if the player is playing brilliantly and grabbing headlines, this could be a great time to do an interview.

As has already been alluded to, interviews are a great way to boost the popularity of a player as well as impress existing and future sponsors. Interviews can take place in a number of different forms, and, in cases where an agent cannot be present (for example a pre- or post-match interview), it is crucial that the intermediary tells their player how to conduct themselves in an appropriate way. Newspaper or magazine interviews are of course much more under your control. Here, it is the agent's responsibility (or in some cases the responsibility of an appointed digital agency) to have prior knowledge of the questions to ensure that the interview goes smoothly and depicts the player in a positive light. This is why having last authorisation on the questions, as well as the power to dictate the article headline, is of paramount importance. The other common types of interview normally take place on social media (perhaps as a live Instagram or Facebook session, or a Twitter Q&A).

Global sporting news outlets

Country	Sports news outlets
England	BBC Sport, Sky Sports, *FourFourTwo* magazine
Germany	*11 Freunde, Kicker*
France	*L'Équipe, France Football*
Spain	*Marca, AS, Sport, Estadio Deportivo*
Italy	*La Gazzetta dello Sport, Corriere dello Sport, Tuttosport*
Portugal	*A Bola, O Jogo, Record*
Netherlands	Voetbalzone, *Voetbal International*, Voetbal Primeur, FC Update
USA	ESPN, Bleacher Report, *Sports Illustrated*

Turkey	*Fanatik, Fotomaç*
Australia	*SBS (The World Game)*, Fox Sports, *The Daily Telegraph*, *Herald Sun*

This list is of course not exhaustive, and most mainstream newspapers have their own influential sports columns that are widely read. When choosing which news outlets would be most beneficial for your player to interview with, it is important to consider the audience which the organisation appeals to, in conjunction with the country or regions that it sells in.

Working with journalists

Knowing which journalists to trust is something that all agents find difficult at some point, and is a part of the profession that you pick up as you go along! As an agent, you will always get calls asking about the future of your clients, with many journalists phrasing the questions in a clever and manipulative way. Therefore, you have to be cautious, as any mistake could be costly. However, this doesn't mean that you should not pursue any relations with journalists, as they can be greatly effective in strengthening your stance as an agent representing a client. Of course, relationships with journalists are quid pro quo, and they'll be looking to get some information back if they help you out – this is totally normal and just how it is! The following scenarios are where journalists can be really important to you and your player:

1. ***Your client wants to move to a new club.*** Use your contact to see if they know information that you may not (e.g. about the club's intentions, or other players moving). Similarly, helping to spread word of the positive impact your player has and their on-pitch performance is something that can be done.

2. ***Your client wants a new contract.*** Much like the above scenario, the media contact can be very useful here. You could come out on behalf of the player, signalling their intentions to stay with their club despite outside interest, and thus help spark some urgency from the club.

3. ***Your client is launching a business.*** Off-pitch ventures are also newsworthy, and if you're trying to promote a new brand or business that your player has launched then use someone in the media to help share information and promote it.

Summary

- The press and mainstream media carry great significance, and work in this field has to be conducted effectively and smartly.
- If you chose to do an interview, make sure it is with the right media outlet at the right time, and, if you start to develop a relationship with a journalist, try to be sure of their loyalty and trustworthiness.
- Much like every other aspect of the profession, you should make sure your client is kept updated about future interviews and press work, as they will have

their own ideas about how they want to be presented to the public.

The expert's view: Rory Smith
(Chief Soccer Correspondent, *New York Times*)

Nothing is quite so treasured by a football journalist as a strong, open, trusting relationship with an agent. That is no surprise. Journalism's prime currency is information, and there are few quite so rich in that as agents. They know if their clients are happy to stay or about to leave a club; they know which players are complaining about the manager and which remain loyal; they have their fingers on the pulse of what is happening throughout the game. Being able to share information with an agent should be the perfect way to make our work more accurate.

It does not always work like that. As a rule, journalists encounter three types of agents. The best are those who are willing to trust you, and to offer an honest reflection of reality as they see it. Second are those who do not engage at all, who will not answer the phone or simply offer a gruff 'No comment'. And third are those who, believing you need them more than they need you, choose to distort the truth to further their own ends.

Even at a time when many players prefer to access their fans directly through social media, there are increasingly few of the latter group. More and more agents recognise that journalists are not the enemy. In an age when players are as much brands as athletes, the media can help to present a true reflection of their clients; they can get their side of the story out in such a way that it does not look like propaganda; they can boost their profile. The cost is not high: just honest answers to a few questions every now and again.

CHAPTER TWELVE

THE OFF-PITCH WORK OF AN AGENT

Whilst a crucial part of the off-pitch work of an agent is in the marketing and social media aspects of the profession, there are many other key duties that have to be carried out with diligence. Even though some of these tasks may seem relatively straightforward, they will often be abandoned by lots of agents who are overly focused on the transfers and contracts side of the job. Remember, the top agents will do more than just negotiate a move from one club to another, and will provide their client with the vast array of services that are needed to manage a footballer nowadays.

Charity

Although something like charity would never appear in a Representation Contract, or even cross most people's minds when thinking about the agency world, it should be recognised that agents have a moral obligation to ensure their client gives back to those less fortunate. A large part of the charity work of a player is closely tied in with their club. Most teams have their own charitable foundation (or at least charities they are close to) that the players will have to help represent. Normally, this takes the form of team visits to hospitals, or hosting sessions for children and young adults at the stadium or training ground. Furthermore, your client might even be asked to be part of a global campaign on behalf of FIFA or UEFA (Union of European Football Associations), which use top players to help promote their charitable endeavours. However, given the influence you have on your player, you must try to make them aware that philanthropic work shouldn't be confined to the required attendance days or visits with clubs or federations, and there are many things that you and your client can do in order to help local and international communities:

1. **Your client has their own foundation.** Perhaps one of the more long-term things to do when it comes to charitable contributions is to set up a foundation in your player's name. Often, if a player has a foundation a family member will run it as the areas and people the foundation hopes to help have a personal importance, but at the same time this will require your input and guidance at all times.

2. **Tickets and memorabilia.** An easier way to give back on a regular basis is through match day experiences or signed gifts. You as the agent could help arrange for a couple of fans from either the club's foundation or another charity to come to watch a game. This

becomes more feasible if your client has a box or suite at the stadium, but if you contact the club they will more than likely assist in finding great seats. Mesut Özil, for example, gives away a third of his box seats to charity each home game. Similarly, giving away signed memorabilia (kits, boots, footballs etc.) is such an easy yet powerful thing that you can push your client to do frequently.

Property

As was briefly mentioned in Chapter 7, one thing that an agent may have to advise on is the living arrangements of the player. Whilst there is no formula for where and how players live, their on-pitch situation does normally dictate what happens. If you're representing a top player who has a stable position at their club, then it makes sense to secure a long-term rent or even purchase a property. Not only is the latter advantageous particularly if the player has (or is planning to start) a family, but also because property can be a good investment. If your player has a growing portfolio of assets, then this can only be seen as positive so long as they maintain their worth in the market. Of course, like any investment, the buying of property is by no means a guaranteed profitable exercise, so do make sure you consult with some experts and lawyers beforehand.

In contrast, most young players will still live with their family, and not want to buy a property in case they are loaned out to another club. Similarly, if your client is only on a short-term contract or looking likely to be transferred, it may be better to just rent. Remember, whatever the footballing situation, it is partially your responsibility to ensure that your player is living comfortably, as this will only benefit their on-pitch performance.

Tax

Whilst being an accountant is by no means part of the required skills of an agent, those who offer a complete service will ensure that their client's money and assets are secure. If you are an agent who is (or aspires to be) doing everything for your player, then making sure they pay their taxes on time and legally is fundamentally important. Simply put, footballers are not above the law, and taxes and bills still have to be paid. There is no shortage of players in the news and media who have allegedly not paid tax or attempted to get around certain rules and regulations. Often, this comes about when certain people approach you, your client or their family, detailing a great plan to save money and reduce the tax bill. At the end of the day you represent the player's best interests, and making sure everything is done legally and properly is always the way to go. Having a really trustworthy and reliable accountant is at the heart of this, and speaking to other reliable agents about who they use is a good way to go about finding one if you are struggling to do so.

Wealth management and investments

Again, being an expert in this isn't a necessity, but closely linked with the idea of developing a personal brand for your client (see Chapter 10) is thinking about how best to utilise your client's wealth to develop long-term financial stability. As the agent, you will no doubt be approached by many people with business proposals, and the decision to pursue any of them is certainly a risk – but this is where great agents can be separated from good agents. Making tough and important decisions is vital in this profession, as is knowing when to say no. When assessing suggestions or making plans for an investment or project that involves your client, a few key considerations have to be made:

1. **Type of brand.** Given that this is not as clear-cut as an endorsement deal, whether or not a player can invest in a company or brand that is a competitor of a principal club sponsor is somewhat of a grey area, and most likely depends on the role of your client in publicly promoting and supporting it. However, one thing that investments have in common with endorsement deals and sponsors is that, whatever this brand does, it directly reflects on your client – good or bad. So, be aware, be smart, and be diligent.

2. **Money.** A key contribution in an investment or new business is the capital the player can provide. Of course, this is entirely down to the player and what they choose to do – even though you can advise, you cannot force them into an arrangement they are not comfortable with. Successful projects and investments occur when the player is fully aware of what their money will be used for, and when they are consulted upon crucial decisions. Whilst they will more than

likely have little to do with the day-to-day operations, it is your duty to keep them updated and informed of what is happening.

3. ***Publicity.*** Don't think that, just because your client has a large social media following, you ***have*** to use it to promote and advertise a brand that they have invested in or are starting up. Remember, every post on their social media channels (ever so slightly) devalues the worth of the page, as it becomes less unique to be featured on it. Even though it is tempting for the player to be constantly 'tagging' or promoting their own projects, there should be some concept of natural growth that doesn't require continual self-advertisement. You never know – your favourite coffee shop, restaurant or product may have a football player behind it!

eSports

One area that is somewhat linked with investments and post-career opportunities is that of eSports. Nowadays there exist eSports 'athletes', who play video games (such as the spinoff ***FIFA*** series) in a professional capacity. Although this concept may seem strange at first, eSports 'athletes', like real footballers, need professional representation as many of them play for teams, which therefore requires contracts (and sometimes transfers!), in addition to marketing. So, in this sense, you could also represent eSports players, alongside your other clients.

However, the way this links in with the ideas discussed in this chapter is that footballers and ex-footballers (as well as those from other sports) are engaging with this new phenomenon in many different ways. Some are investing in eSports companies and teams, whilst others (like Mesut Özil) have built their own professional squad that plays competitively. Although this market is still quite small, it is estimated to see huge growth in the coming years, and therefore could present a good off-pitch opportunity for your client in whatever capacity.

Summary

- It is clear that the power and global reach of football present a multitude of opportunities for players and agents alike away from the football pitch.
- Always try to think one step ahead of everybody else – in planning projects and making key decisions, consider the short, medium and long term where possible.
- Never forget that football is a powerful profession, and as an agent you hold lots of responsibility and sway. Make sure you use this wisely, and in the best possible way.

The expert's view: Daniel Ross (Managing Partner, Ross Bennet Smith Chartered Accountants)

This book does a great job at demonstrating that football is no longer confined to a ninety-minute match once or twice a week. Football is a major industry, with footballers needing representation in all areas; when it comes to financial matters it is no different.

In an industry awash with money it's remarkable

how many examples there are of successful players left penniless, going bankrupt or being convicted of offences such as tax fraud. These issues don't just impact the professional footballer, but also their agents, with negative perception potentially diminishing the value of the player in question and their brand.

Rather than the agent assuming responsibility for dealing with financial and tax matters, which are often far more complex than they might appear and requiring specific expertise, relationships with professional and trusted advisors, such as accountants, should be actively encouraged and certainly not feared.

Given that football is an industry with many unique idiosyncrasies it's important when appointing an accountant for a player to ensure that they can do more than just file a tax return. A good accountant should be able to add a great deal of value across a wide range of financial matters and be familiar with the industry, multi-jurisdictional tax structuring, image rights, endorsements and VAT, as well as being able to provide around-the-clock general financial advice and assist with foreign exchange, investments, mortgages and banking matters.

As the Managing Partner of Ross Bennet Smith Chartered Accountants, a firm that has been acting for top-flight footballers across the world for over 25 years, I've worked with a wide variety of agents. Those agents I would consider to the best all seem to have one thing in common, which is rather than attempting to be 'all things to all men', they will instead build a team around their players with each member having the appropriate and specific expertise, thereby making it easier to ensure that a footballers needs and objectives are met.

CHAPTER THIRTEEN

THE SECOND CAREER OF A FOOTBALL PLAYER

(Written in conjunction with Stéphane Ehrhart. After a playing and coaching career, Stéphane is now working with UEFA and specialises in the transition of footballers from playing to post-career opportunities. With over twelve years of experience, Stéphane has worked on high-profile projects and is himself an author.)

The average duration of a European professional footballer's career is only five years. Additionally, 40% of players declare bankruptcy after five years of being in retirement. These numbers are alarming, and it is clear that the next generation of agents need to be working with their clients not just when they are playing but long after too. The famous footballers who have been incredibly well remunerated throughout their career only represent a tiny proportion of the reality. For 80% of players, their career ends prematurely because of injury or the inability to find another contract. That is why planning the 'second career' of your client is pivotal. Having projects and ventures already in motion before their retirement day comes is something that the best agents will have done.

Facing the reality of retirement

One thing that is unavoidable for a footballer is that one day it will come to an end. No matter how talented, famous or successful you are, there will be a day when their career will have to stop… and it will hurt. As such, players will normally encounter three major changes in their lives:

1. ***Physical change.*** Former players are no longer required to train every day, and as such their bodies will burn fewer calories and will face a serious lack of the dopamine and adrenaline which came from the competition and playing. Suddenly, the meals provided by the club at training no longer exist, and their diet will differ.

2. ***Psychological change.*** Usually, players will miss their teammates, the banter and camaraderie that went with being with the same people day in, day out. Similarly, they might be recognised in the streets less often, they'll be less talked about on a regular basis, and they may feel less relevant. The same goes for those close to them. Their entourage, spouse, children and friends might all be subject to the same change, sometimes

resulting in periods of depression, burnout or sadness, or leading to divorce.

3. **Logistical change.** Most of the times, when a football career comes to an end, the player and their family will relocate to a new city, or a new house. This means that the whole family environment and routine will completely change. Of course, it's inevitable that the level of income will also decrease, which might force the family to change their spending habits, thereby creating additional pressures and tensions.

Combined, these factors clearly demonstrate the vast change that retirement brings to a football player. They also show that a player (and therefore their agent) has to start thinking about what happens next long before retirement comes.

Going about a player's second career

Each player, agent and family member will have their own ideas about how to go about post-career opportunities, and whilst all situations do differ there is a generic method that can be followed. Depending on what exactly you do with your client, it is still always a good idea to work hand in hand with professionals in order to prepare players properly and offer them the best possible advice, support and training. The following advice can certainly be of benefit when exploring this area:

1. ***Avoiding mistakes and protecting funds.*** Making sure you prepare your player for their life after football is crucial. Therefore, you have to give advice and guidance in terms of managing (or at least safeguarding) their wealth. This idea was touched upon in the previous chapter, but, put simply, if your client has spent a large part of their income on material items, this leaves very little to pursue business opportunities once they have retired.

2. ***Who to involve.*** The specifics of each player and agent can obviously differ vastly, but as already mentioned, having somebody else working closely alongside the agent for such ventures can be beneficial. There could be someone you (or your client) already have in mind. Alternatively, this is why networking and having a good reach of contacts is vital, as you'll meet experts and professionals all the time. The earlier you find the right partners the better, as it will give the player time to see that the people involved with their post-playing career are trustworthy, solid and reliable. Organisations such as Afterfoot are prominent in this field, as well as UEFA and some national associations.

3. ***Timing.*** Often, because of the stark changes to their lives as described previously, ex-players will waste a lot of time between the end of their football career and the start of their 'second career'. Consequently, they can get frustrated if things aren't moving quickly enough and will lose patience and confidence in the project. This is why it is always advantageous if the projects and ventures pursued post career are started

while the player is still playing. Besides the benefits just mentioned, an active player has an audience and fanbase who are still engaged, which gives the projects a bigger platform.

Football-related opportunities

Whilst what has been discussed thus far relates to business ventures away from the pitch, there are still plenty of ways to get your client paid footballing opportunities even after retirement. As the following table indicates, many well-known players from the previous generation of stars have become managers or pundits, or have worked with clubs in various capacities. Whilst the advantages of being close to a manager or club official have already been explained (see Chapter 6), yet to be covered is your role once your player has retired and is planning to transition into a different job post career. Say, for example, you represent a footballer who wants to work as a pundit and analyst for a TV channel. Much like with a player moving from one club to another, these things require discussions and negotiations to take place, all resulting in an eventual deal. Similarly, before a retired player can become a manager, they have to gain experience in coaching and obtain badges and certificates. Essentially, you would be the one to enquire on your client's behalf and get precise details and information about the next steps.

Although one would be correct in assuming that a player's endorsement and sponsorship value reduces post retirement, this doesn't mean that these types of deals cannot be done. In fact, they are far easier given the lack of contractual obligations and restrictions that come with an Employment Contract, and that the player obviously has much more time to devote to the deal.

Player	Current role
John Terry	Coach, Aston Villa
Frank Lampard	Manager, Derby County
Steven Gerrard	Manager, Rangers
Phil Neville	Manager, England women's team
Gary Neville	Pundit
Jamie Carragher	Pundit
Jamie Redknapp	Pundit
David Beckham	Co-owner, Inter Miami FC; Salford City
Edwin van der Sar	CEO, AFC Ajax
Eric Abidal	Director of Football, Barcelona
Maxwell	Assistant Sporting Director, Paris Saint-Germain
Kaspars Gorkšs	President, Latvian Football Federation
Jason Roberts	Director of Development, CONCACAF

Correct as of January 2019

Summary

- If you want continued success in this profession, then working with players once they have retired is a great opportunity to achieve this.
- Working with the right partner and associate who can elevate the ventures pursued in your client's second career is important, and you should be looking for people with shared values of trust and loyalty.
- As with any aspect of the profession, making sure the player is aware of your plans and what you're doing is key – being open and honest is the only way to ensure your client's trust.

CHAPTER FOURTEEN

A HISTORY OF THE PROFESSION

Perhaps not commonly thought of as a profession with much history, the football agent industry does in fact have a fairly rich and intriguing past. Given how the sport has gone from not needing agents to relying on them heavily in everyday practice, the rapid increase in the importance of the agent is in large part due to advancements made in the mid-1990s. During this time, agents became officially recognised by FIFA, and the crucial court case that took place in 1995 (the Bosman ruling) completely revolutionised the business. Nevertheless, the roots of the business began well before this date, and can be traced back to the late 1800s, from when certain aspects of intermediary activity are evident in surviving records.

The early years

During the nineteenth century there was really no such thing as a football agent, although this did not stop J.P. Campbell from submitting an article to the English newspaper *Athletic News* in 1891, looking for young footballing talent. Nevertheless, despite Campbell's publication, the active participation of an intermediary regarding a transfer or contract was unheard of.

Decades later, in the 1930s, it was clear that football had to reflect the politics and international relations of the era, with nearly all the major European football associations placing limits (or even bans) on the transfer of foreign players. Whilst the FFF fought hard to counter these decisions, the very concept of a football agent was in doubt as it heavily relied upon the prospect of transfers, which were sparse at this time. However, hope for intermediaries still existed in Europe, and similarities to today can be pinpointed. In Italy, the establishment of a transfer market gave birth to talks between club owners and directors, as well as intermediaries, with such discussions over players often taking place at the Gallia Hotel in Milan. Therefore, it is clear that this was a time in which intermediary activity was developing, yet in general the agency profession was mostly limited.

Representation of football players

Despite there being strict regulations regarding transfers, and therefore agents, the desire across Europe to create better football clubs, coupled with increasing political cooperation post World War II, started to enable the growth of prominent intermediaries. The first of this new breed was Gigi Peronace, who specialised in transfers between the English and Italian leagues. He played a key role in many groundbreaking deals at the time, including John Charles (Leeds United to Juventus), Jimmy Greaves (Chelsea to AC Milan) and Denis Law (Manchester City to Torino), earning him notability and success.

Years later, agents started to understand the commercial opportunities that could accompany their clients' fame. After his transfer to Hamburg in 1977, Kevin Keegan and his representatives signed football's first 'face deal'. This contract, nowadays known as an Image Rights Agreement, enabled him to become one of the most instantly recognisable celebrities via promoting any product that came his way. Consequently, Keegan quickly became a valuable asset for any agent, and set the precedent for future deals and proceedings.

Recognition by FIFA

With football agents becoming more and more prominent in the sport, it was inevitable that formal recognition would happen. In 1994, FIFA finally implemented the first set of rules and regulations regarding agents, which in turn made football agency a formal profession. This meant that football federations across the world now had guidelines on how to become a licensed agent, thus heralding the beginning of the modern intermediary, whose role and power greatly increased within the sport.

The Bosman ruling

Whilst 1994 was clearly a pivotal year for football agents, the following year, 1995, was equally important, as the Bosman ruling would shape the way football worked, and still plays a crucial part in the sport today. The court ruling meant that a player could move to a new club without their former team receiving a transfer fee. As a result, agents could demand larger salaries for their clients and, consequently, larger commissions for themselves. An example of this can be seen just four years after the rule was implemented. Steve McManaman became the highest-paid British footballer when he moved from Liverpool to Real Madrid at the end of his contract. This way of thinking remains exactly the same today, with 'free agents' (as they are now called) a very common method of transfer that is often exploited by intermediaries.

The following table gives some further examples of the Bosman ruling being implemented:

Player	Country	Year	Transfer
Edgar Davids	Netherlands	1996	Ajax → AC Milan
Steve McManaman	England	1999	Liverpool → Real Madrid
Brad Friedel	United States of America	2000	Tottenham Hotspur → Blackburn
Sol Campbell	England	2001	Tottenham Hotspur → Arsenal
Henrik Larsson	Sweden	2004	Celtic → Barcelona
Esteban Cambiasso	Argentina	2004	Real Madrid → Inter Milan

Michael Ballack	Germany	2006	Bayern Munich → Chelsea
David Beckham	England	2007	Real Madrid → LA Galaxy
Andrea Pirlo	Italy	2011	AC Milan → Juventus
Robert Lewand-owski	Poland	2014	Borussia Dortmund → Bayern Munich
Zlatan Ibrahimović	Sweden	2016	Paris Saint-Germain → Manchester United
Sead Kolašinac	Bosnia and Herzegovina	2017	Schalke 04 → Arsenal
Emre Can	Germany	2018	Liverpool → Juventus
Gianluigi Buffon	Italy	2018	Juventus → Paris Saint-Germain
Jack Wilshere	England	2018	Arsenal → West Ham United
Andrés Iniesta	Spain	2018	Barcelona → Vissel Kobe

Source: Transfermarkt (correct as of January 2019)

Summary

- Although knowing about the history of the profession is not a prerequisite for success in the industry, the past is something that all football agents have in common.
- Events in the mid-1990s were pivotal in the creation of the modern intermediary, as football agency was given both recognition and power.
- The Bosman ruling paved the way for a type of transfer that gives agents the advantage over clubs when a player's contract is coming to its end, with such cases being pertinent to this day.

The expert's view: Jörg Neubauer
(Agent of Leon Goretzka and Kevin Trapp)

I started working in the field of football agency in 1990, at a time when the profession was limited to helping broker deals. However, during that time I began to understand that a player needs more than just someone who can negotiate a contract. As a result, I started to learn about areas such as tax and insurance, legal advice, public relations and press activities – many of which now seem like necessities for the agency business. For me, this was the step towards the professionalisation of player consulting. In addition, it was clear that there was a huge transformation occurring – something I describe as the 'transparency of footballers'. Thanks to the internet, social media and data collection, there is absolutely no room for secrets any more. Nowadays, everything is public and easy to access – this represents the most fundamental shift in the business over the last twenty-five years.

The football market has always been interesting and the game itself has undergone its own individual development. Nevertheless, the greatest steps taken have not been towards sporting success, but rather regarding monetary terms. The huge increase in commercialisation within football, especially through increased income outside of the stadium (such as from broadcasting rights and sponsorships), means there is more money available. Consequently, there has been the aforementioned change in the nature of football agency. Whereas during the 1990s an agent was an individual, today agencies are in the majority, and this has somewhat led to the disappearance of the individual within the industry. As a pioneer in this field, at the end of the 1990s I started to establish a scouting network for young players, and with a scout I was able to find the best talent. This area also showed rapid development: similar to football clubs, the agencies started to build their own national and international scouting systems. The result was that the growth of a player started much younger.

To sum up, this business has gone through an enormous transition since I started out in it. Despite this, one thing has remained constant: the agent who represents the best players is the agent who does the best business.

CHAPTER FIFTEEN

'SHOW ME THE MONEY'

As in any profession, money is always a crucial factor when deciding whether to pursue a career in football agency or not. The positive thing with football is that there is certainly no shortage of money! With the ever-expanding commercialisation of the football industry, transfers and contracts remain high. But the opportunities don't stop there. Given the huge reach of football, the ideas discussed about projects and ventures, as well as ownership and mergers and acquisitions, are all areas in which you can get involved.

Wages

Your constant source of income comes from the Representation and Employment Contracts you have agreed with your client. These entitle you to your agreed commission and agent's fee, which are normally paid to you by the club itself. This is because they typically pay on behalf of the player. Although a small percentage of someone else's wages seems like a bad deal, football is like very few other professions! It is estimated that the total European wage bill for footballers is around £9.5 billion per year and thus there is certainly room for you to take a slice of this huge and growing market. Using all the skills and connections that you have formed, it is up to you to negotiate the best possible deal for your client, and in turn make yourself more money.

Transfers

With wages offering you a steady flow of money, transfers provide an alternative source of income for you as an agent. Whether you have a mandate for a player's transfer, or you are their registered agent, there is potential to make a large sum of money when your client moves to a new club. More often than not, the transfer includes a set fee for the agent as a commission for brokering the deal. More and more clubs are willing to pay intermediaries due to the increased pressure for success, and they know how important agents are in getting a deal done. This is evidenced by the fact that Premier League clubs spent just over £260 million on combined agents' fees in the 2018–19 season. Yet this high level of agency payments isn't confined to the top division of each country. Using England as an example, Championship clubs paid £50 million to agents (which represents an £8 million increase). Likewise, League One clubs spent £5.5 million in the same period, with League Two also contributing just under £1 million. Although England may not be the most representative of the norm, it still goes to show the money in the industry throughout the divisions.

Club	Estimated spending 2018–19	Estimated agent spending 2018–19
AFC Bournemouth	£80.19m	£10,295,433
Arsenal	£73.35m	£11,181,730
Brighton & Hove Albion	£77.63m	£6,859,429
Burnley	£29.7m	£3,975,928
Cardiff	£46.08m	£2,802,375
Chelsea	£189m	£26,850,552
Crystal Palace	£10.67m	£6,976,425
Everton	£89.82m	£19,116,370
Fulham	£100.80m	£8,234,360
Huddersfield Town	£45.63m	£5,023,807
Leicester City	£103.14m	£12,720,618
Liverpool	£163.98m	£43,795,863
Manchester City	£69.38m	£24,122,753
Manchester United	£74.43m	£20,759,350
Newcastle United	£53.78m	£8,868,027
Southampton	£56.03m	£6,151,107
Tottenham Hotspur	£0	£11,141,255
Watford	£27.09m	£10,894,179
West Ham United	£94.82m	£14,414,845
Wolves	£101.03m	£6,479,714
Total	£1.486bn	£260,664,118

Source: Transfermarkt, BBC Sport

Other projects

Another way in which an agent can make money is through other projects, which are inherently linked with their existing clients. Due to the power and attraction that football players have, they can easily open doors for agents to pursue further business ventures. As discussed in Chapter 12, all the potential projects mentioned require the agent to be present and active, from making sure your client's investment and brand are protected to finding suitable partners and ways to make it all a success. The types of projects are crucial to your income as well, as the agent will often get some shares in the business, which will give you (as well as the player) a source of income post retirement.

Ownership and M&A (mergers and acquisitions)

Another area in which agents can get involved is the more business-related side of clubs. If you're an agent who is determined to expand your network as far and wide as possible, you may cross paths with extremely wealthy business people wanting to get into the world of football. You may therefore be lucky enough one day to be part of a deal for a takeover of a club. When partnering with an affluent business person, they may use you in order to help put together the deal (i.e. you will act as an intermediary for the takeover of the club), and may even give you shares in the team as a result.

If this opportunity comes to you, it is a clear sign of your success and something you will have to contemplate.

One thing to note, though, is what the regulations have to say about this, and it is certainly a grey area. There is an obvious conflict of interests if an agent part-owns a club that has one of their players in the squad! Yet there is less of a clear-cut ruling on an agent brokering the takeover of a club, without receiving any shares. As just mentioned, this is an ill-defined area of football, and could well be subject to more rigorous regulations in the future.

Summary

- Whilst it shouldn't be the main motivating factor, the money available for you to make by being an intermediary is enticing and by no means unrealistic.
- The commission that you receive from representing a client can be your only source of income, but not capitalising on the business opportunities that stem from the player's popularity is a missed opportunity.
- Yet there is a strong distinction to be made between good business and simply taking advantage of your player's fame and wealth – you ought to be open, honest and transparent, as well as always incorporating your client within the business, if you decide to pursue off-pitch work.

The expert's view: Pere Guardiola (Director, Media Base Sports)

I am fortunate enough to have had the opportunity of working in the sports business for many years now. One of the most important things you should know is that football is such a big industry and the possibilities for making money are endless. So if you don't have contacts to get you an internship at a large agency, or a friend who is playing professionally, it doesn't matter.

There are many ways to make a successful living in the football industry. Of course, there are the better-known methods, as already mentioned in this book, such as transfers (in which you can work on either the club's side or the player's – or in some cases both) and commercial deals for your client. Additionally, there are further opportunities relating to football itself, such as M&A (mergers and acquisitions), where you can use the network you have to put together a club looking to sell and an investor looking to buy, taking a percentage of the total sale as your commission or introductory fee.

Moreover, away from the pitch, you can advise your client(s) on investments in a range of industries, including, for example, restaurants and coffee shops. Subsequently, you would be entitled to take a share in the business as your commission. The same can also be said for property and other tangible investments.

Remember, the opportunities that present themselves to you in this business are extremely valuable. Take them and use them wisely, then the money will come to you!

CHAPTER SIXTEEN

'GLOBAL VIEWS'

Australia: Paddy Dominguez
(Owner, Republic Sports Management)

Modern-day football management is very much an international business. Although, as with any business, there are varying levels through which an agent can progress, generally, a football agent will commence working in their local domestic market and grow to gain experience and knowledge of other international territories with time, and an ever-expanding list of clients who will transfer between leagues. Purely from a business perspective, a football agent is effectively, and needs to be, heavily involved in the import/export trade. The global nature of the football industry means that most agents will encounter transfers between different leagues worldwide at some point in their career.

With this in mind, it is important for football agents to be up to date on FIFA regulations as they relate to international transfers. The vast majority of agents over time will build a network, and work in partnership with other agents who have local knowledge. Some of the benefits of utilising local agents and their knowledge in this kind of relationship are:

1. Local agents will know the pay structures of the clubs in their territory.
2. Local agents will have existing relationships with clubs in their respective region.
3. Local agents will know of any anomalies in terms of rules and regulations. *
4. Local agents will have existing relationships with local media.
5. Local agents will be able to advise on lifestyle choices for the player.
6. Local agents can provide day-to-day assistance for the player on the ground.

Currently there are only two salary-capped leagues in world football: the A-League (Australia) and Major League Soccer or the MLS (North America). This creates a unique environment for agents working in these territories as the limits on finances create a market where players' salaries fall into certain categories, which is a natural default position

---

*   There can be some additional regulations in certain territories such as Australia, the USA etc., although all of the fundamental FIFA rules and regulations are adopted by member associations.

based on the number of players in each squad and the limit of the salary cap. Clubs in these countries will have an unofficial range of salary for players in each position. For example, defenders can earn in the range of $250,000–400,000 maximum, midfielders $300,000–450,000 etc. These leagues will generally provide a set number of exemptions for marquee players, who will be considered outside the cap. The rationale behind these players receiving an exemption is based on their value in driving marketing, publicity, attendances and general interest in their respective league.

The Australian A-League is predominantly a feeder league in the global sense of where it stands. One of the youngest leagues in the world (commenced in 2005), it continues to mature season by season and almost all of the best players in this league have the aim of transferring to other clubs in Europe or Asia. Consistently there is debate around whether the salary cap promotes the export of players from this league as footballers can earn a lot more in leagues in which players are not paid within a salary cap structure.

Australian players technically qualify as Asian players, and as such they are very attractive to clubs in the Asian market. The diverse heritage of most Australian families also permits many Australian players access to European passports, and therefore they qualify as European and the Continent, in turn, is the other main destination for players from Australia.

In such a vast country with cities spread far apart it is critical for any agent to build a strong scouting network to identify talent. It is simply impossible for any football agent to scout everywhere, although there are only ten teams in the A-League and this makes it far easier to track players in the top professional league in the country.

Australia has a proud tradition in exporting quality players to Europe, mainly England, Scotland, the Netherlands and Italy. The general pathway, historically, for most Australian players has been through the national team. As Australia has appeared at every World Cup since 2006, and the stature of the national team has continued to grow, it has naturally provided a platform for the best players from Australia to get noticed and impress overseas clubs. As the A-League continues to improve this will allow players from this territory another pathway to seek overseas opportunities.

South America: Matthieu Rios-Grossin (Owner, Alinea Sports Management)

As in all businesses, it is very important to identify the party you will negotiate with. It is also vital to understand what their interests and objectives are so you can be in control of the negotiation. It may sound easy and straightforward, but its importance can't be underestimated, as a deal can become extremely complicated if you don't identify the aims of the club/entity you're negotiating with.

You can see the significance of the above advice when applied to a practical example:

1.   As an agent, you are asked by a club to check on a South American player and construct a deal, or you

want to get a mandate from a player and their agent/club to move them to a European club.

2.   You can ask the player who their agent is and usually they will tell you the agent's name or say that they have no agent.

3.   Despite this, you will sometimes see that the player has signed mandates with different people, and in the middle of a negotiation someone you have never heard of will work their way into the conversation staking their claim in the deal.

4.   If this is the case, it is important that you immediately get all the documents authorising **your** action before you move forward in order to validate yourself to all the parties involved. In fact, getting all the documentation as early in the process as possible is best procedure.

When compared to Europe, the industry in South America operates totally differently. In Europe, people are used to a player having a contract with a club and a full-time agent, so it is easy to know who to contact and negotiate with. However, it is far from this straightforward in South America. Often, the club the player is contracted to will share 'economic rights' (sometimes referred to as ownership) with former clubs, agents, and companies who have helped pay relevant bills.

Of course, this is neither legal nor official as it goes against all the third-party ownership rules and regulations. People cover it up by referring to them as 'private contracts' (frequently with political motivations) that are not disclosed to the football associations. Therefore, you will have to battle against vested interests, personal conflicts, egos etc. when trying to get a deal done.

If you manage to get through all of this, it probably means you have gained the trust of the buying club by simplifying this unfavourable situation, and can now look to proceed with the deal! Now, just make sure everything is legally sound and all the numbers and percentages add up, and double-check all the paperwork.

North America: Costa Smyrniotis (Director & Agent, Axia)

Football in North America is definitely on the rise, with the game constantly growing in both the sporting and commercial aspects. And, with the 2026 World Cup set to be hosted by Canada, the USA and Mexico, even better days can be expected for the sport here.

Liga MX in Mexico and Major League Soccer (MLS) in the United States are the clear leaders from a club competition standpoint in the region. They attract not only the top domestic talent but also a very good quality of international signings. One need not to look any further than the transfer business of the region's top clubs like Tigres, Monterrey, Atlanta United and Toronto FC. In 2019, Canada will also see the launch of a brand-new domestic league competition – the Canadian Premier League – with the goal of joining Liga MX and MLS as the continent's top leagues.

The aforementioned addition shows a healthy and growing landscape in which agents can do quality business for all sorts of clients. Similar to other markets around the world, this region includes a few large organisations with agents working under one umbrella, collectively managing a vast array of players. However, this isn't exclusively the case. There are also many smaller (and more niche) agencies that focus on providing a far more holistic and detailed service for their clients.

Whilst formally starting out as an agent has few requirements beyond the regulations of FIFA and the relevant national associations, there are some unique challenges to working in this market that all prospective agents should be aware of.

For a start, the sheer size of the United States alone is in itself something to consider. Added to this is that the MLS also operates in cities in Canada as well as the US. Many agents in European countries like England, Germany and France have the luxury of being able to cover multiple clubs across many leagues with ease. Even if it means crossing borders, it can still be done without much hassle. However, in America it is obviously far more difficult to be in all places at once. As such, agents should try to focus on becoming an expert in their local region and market first. This can include having a good grasp of the local academies (where top talent comes from) and also building relationships with the clubs in the area (or nearby). This can allow for a solid foundation from which to grow.

If you are travelling across the country, it is best to pick out some top events and games in the yearly calendar to attend. This can be to view development academy tournaments, CONCACAF Youth Championships (U17 and U20), the MLS Combine, the MLS All-Star Game, and Cup Finals. These are excellent networking opportunities and offer the chance to see many players and clubs all in one location.

It is also important for domestic agents to become quite familiar with the unique intricacies of contracts and roster rules prevalent in the domestic competitions they operate in. This is especially true for the MLS, where terms like 'DPs', 'TAM', 'GAM', 'allocation', 'trades', 'home-grown' and 'CBA' are the norm but can leave someone from the outside scratching their head in confusion as to what it all means!

For agents looking to sign a player to an MLS team, remember that the contract is between the player and the league, and **not directly with the club** as is the norm elsewhere in world football. Furthermore, agents should be prepared to deal with standard player contracts governed by league roster rules and collective bargaining agreements between all parties involved. It is certainly a lot to take in and learn from the outset, but by gaining all this knowledge and experience over time agents will be able to best guide players through this environment and negotiate and structure contracts to their maximum possible benefit.

For foreign agents looking to find an opportunity for one of their players in North America, it is suggested to find a reputable local partner who is a market expert with deep knowledge, experience and established connections with clubs. This is especially true in light of the unique contractual and roster rules mentioned above. In addition, they can best assist by being closer to the player and providing valuable support 'on the ground' with the many off-pitch requirements that are so crucial in today's game. Of course, with such a relationship the flip side is also true when the time comes for a player to move out of North America to another region.

Asia: Dee Hong
(Head of International Affairs, Footballade)

The life of an agent in Korea may not differ much from that of my counterparts in Europe or elsewhere in the world. I start my day with a cup of coffee and check my phone to navigate through emails, news, Instagram and other social media channels to see what the football world has to offer. On a weekly basis I attend matches, speak with my players and chat with some club authorities whenever possible.

The movie *Jerry Maguire* inspired me the most and attracted me to get a foothold in the football industry. However, in this profession nothing comes easy. It takes a long time for any agent to establish themselves, and I was no different! I was very lucky with my background, as I worked with the Korean FA, sponsors and clubs, enabling me to get valuable experience. The only missing piece to complete the puzzle was working with the players directly, and I'm proud to finally be able to have that opportunity now. Even though I am still a newbie, my previous experiences have really helped me since I'm now acquainted with many important and interesting people in the industry, whilst also gaining crucial interactive skills. I am certainly not the first (and definitely will not be the last) to state how vital it is to establish this network of contacts in the football world.

In recent years the Korean football industry has had to compete with its financially superior neighbours in Japan and China. Since the Korean game is played at a very high level within the region, the infrastructure and surrounding environment will hopefully keep improving and match the strong sportive performance. In doing so, this opportunity may serve to boost the business surrounding football.

In order to make the most of this increase in funding and infrastructure, more transfers to different countries or continents have to be executed. Although language barriers may delay the process, the more we try the better we will become. The region remains a learning curve for the whole industry, but eventually it will benefit the market in general.

We have had some fantastic players over the years, including Son, Ki, Park and Lee in our national team line-up. I hope that in the near future Korea could also introduce a Sögüt who can represent high-calibre players. My ultimate goal as a football agent is to fulfil my clients' dreams while also keeping the fans entertained.

Africa: Yussif Alhassan Chibsah (CEO & Founder, Club Consult Africa)

Introduction

I have been surrounded by football nearly my whole life! Being an ex-professional footballer, I was fortunate enough to have played for all the various national teams of Ghana from the youth to senior level. I captained the Ghanaian

Olympic football team (Black Meteors) at the Athens Olympic Games in 2004, and I was also a member of the Black Stars squad in the lead up to the 2006 World Cup in Germany.

At club level, I played professional football in Italy, Finland, Germany, Israel, Sweden and Turkey. Among all these countries, Sweden was where I played the longest, with ten years of professional football there in total.

Whilst playing, I started to mentor young African players in the Sweden and other Scandinavia countries (Denmark, Finland and Norway), acting as a role model and giving any advice or help I could.

My educational background was in banking and finance, and it had been my intention to practise this after my footballing career had come to an end. However, some of the young African players I was mentoring suggested that I become an agent and representative.

Football agency in Africa is certainly behind the European industry. I therefore felt the worry and pain of these young players, and when I thought about how different I felt playing in Africa compared to Europe, I decided it was better to work on improving the agency business in my home continent.

I decided to use all that I have learnt in Europe as a professional footballer and the experience I have gathered from all agents I encountered to help those back home in Africa.

The industry in Africa

Before the introduction of the intermediary system, there were very few licensed FIFA agents in Ghana and across

Africa, and even those that were licensed tended to be based in Europe.

Back then there was an exam, and this deterred a lot of people, but at the same time gave the profession perhaps a higher standard of intermediary due to the restrictive nature of the system.

Either way, the agency world in Africa has huge potential. There is an abundance of footballing talent across the continent that could really benefit from high-level representation.

How the industry operated

Because there were few licensed agents around, the industry operated through local people who called themselves the 'managers' of players. These people were not licensed, but essentially played the role of agents and did everything for the player, whether it be acting as their guardian, or providing sponsorship. This could be in the form of giving them football boots, training kits or a monthly allowance.

In exchange for these services, they would become the decision-maker for the players. Domestic clubs would have to contact them if they need the services of the players. They get paid either by the buying club or the player, and, even though these 'managers' have no licence to operate, the system accepted them. Essentially therefore, they operated as agents for a very long time.

Players with a bad character and attitude will keep changing their 'managers' any time they want to, by jumping from one rich person to another. The one with the highest bid always wins, as there is no proper structure or regulation in the system. Some 'managers' did very well for themselves with good returns on their investments, whilst others lost out heavily.

But at the end of the day, there is no loyalty in this system. Players will tend to just ignore their 'manager' when a European agent comes along with interest from a European club.

Similarly, there is no professionalism. In Africa, some players do not even know the duration of their contracts, nor how much they earn per month.

Scouting

There are also some differences when it comes to scouting in Africa. The negative part is that there lacks structure and regulation. One can visit any game, identify a talent and straightaway become the representative of the player, especially in cases where the 'manager' involved is rich. Due to the fact that most domestic clubs do not have the finances to operate a youth side, they rely on these 'managers' to provide them with young talent because they don't have to invest in them.

Often, small tournaments are organised which have some of the top players from the best clubs. These events are organised by both local and European agents, as well as clubs, foreign club representatives, and 'managers'. Subsequently, these players are offered to the European teams.

Introduction of the intermediary system

The introduction of the various FIFA regulations has brought about a little bit of structure, but still more work needs to be done!

In my own opinion, the system of allowing individual federations to have the power and control is an issue in Africa, because the associations are more interested in the intermediary fee they collect rather than the standard of the industry. Almost every football fan became an intermediary because all they needed to do is to register. Family members and friends of footballers all became intermediaries without any technical knowledge of the game, and many talents are misled because of a lack of knowledge. All they are interested in is the money.

That is why education is so key!

Personally, I think we need greater education and regulation to improve the agency business in Africa. Right now we have many fraudsters who registered as intermediaries and all they do is go onto the internet and pull pictures of famous managers and agents, create Photoshops, and deceive players by claiming they are partners with these big names. The promise of a 'big contract' means many fall for their tricks. Players who are so desperate to play in Europe are victim of these plans, and as such lose money and opportunities.

At the end of the day, the system is currently failing the players. It is them that are losing out, as innocent talent is being deceived. There needs to be change, and, as I said before, education and regulation are two key components of what the future should be like!

CHAPTER SEVENTEEN

EXAMPLE CONTRACTS

England: FA (Football Association)
Representation Contract

STANDARD REPRESENTATION CONTRACT between
INTERMEDIARY and PLAYER

THIS STANDARD REPRESENTATION CONTRACT
('THE CONTRACT') is made BETWEEN

NAME OF INTERMEDIARY: ....
(the 'Intermediary') of: ....
COMPANY NAME (where applicable): ....
ADDRESS: ....
NAME OF PLAYER (the 'Player'): ....
ADDRESS: ....
DATE OF BIRTH: ....

IT IS HEREBY AGREED as follows:

APPOINTMENT
1.   The Intermediary is appointed by the Player to provide services on the following terms:

   ....

DURATION
2.   The Contract shall take effect on ....
   and will terminate on ....
   (maximum two years) without notice.

EXCLUSIVITY
3.   The Player is contracted to the Intermediary on:
   an exclusive basis   ☐
   a non-exclusive basis   ☐

REMUNERATION
4.   The Player shall pay to the Intermediary a commission amounting to .... %
   of the Player's Basic Gross Income as a result of any Employment Contract negotiated or renegotiated by the Intermediary, payable as follows:
*   *a lump sum payment at the start*
      of the Employment Contract   ☐
*   *annual payments at the end of each contractual year* ☐
*   *other (specify):* .... ☐

(No remuneration will be due to the Intermediary while the Player remains a Minor)

TERMINATION

5. The Contract shall be automatically terminated with immediate effect if the Intermediary's Registration expires during the term of the Contract and the Intermediary does not renew his Registration within 14 days of being requested to do so in writing by the Player.

SUPPLEMENTAL TERMS AND CONDITIONS

6. Any other arrangements between the parties in any way connected to the provision of the services set out in Clause 1 that are supplemental to the Contract shall be in accordance with the requirements of the FA Regulations on Working with Intermediaries and the FIFA Regulations on Working with Intermediaries, and must be attached to the Contract and lodged with the FA together with the Contract.

DISPUTES

7. Any dispute between the parties arising out of or in connection with the Contract, including but not limited to any question regarding its existence, validity or termination, shall be referred to and finally resolved by arbitration under Rule K of the Rules of the FA (as amended from time to time).

GOVERNING LAW

8. The Contract and any non-contractual obligation arising out of or in connection to it are governed by and shall be construed in accordance with the laws of

England and Wales and subject to Clause 6 above. The parties hereby submit to the exclusive jurisdiction of the courts of England and Wales.

SIGNATURES
A copy of the Contract has been provided to the Player and lodged with the FA.

Signed by the Player: ....
Date: ....

Signed by the Guardian: ....
Date: ....
(if the Player is a Minor)

Print Name: ....

Signed by/on behalf of the Intermediary: ....
Date: ....

Print Name: ....

Germany: DFB (Deutscher Fußball-Bund) Intermediary Application Form

---

In accordance with § 3, no. 2 or 3 (as applicable) of the DFB Regulations on Working with Intermediaries,
I/we (Player/Club)   ....
would like to register the Intermediary specified below.

Name of Intermediary: ....

I/We enclose the following documentation:
*   ☐ the signed Intermediary Declaration for natural and/or legal persons in accordance with Annexes I and 2 of the Regulations, as well as
*   ☐ the signed Representation Contract. (Except: ☐ Contract has already been submitted to the DFL.)

The Intermediary has stated to have already been registered with the DFB:

☐ Yes   ☐ No

If the above Intermediary has not yet been duly registered as such with the DFB, I/we also enclose:
*   ☐ a Certificate of Good Conduct (or its foreign equivalent) in accordance with the provisions of § 2, no. 2, par. 2. (Except: ☐ The Intermediary has stated to have submitted such a document to the DFB in the season before.)

- □ as well as the Intermediary's contact details as provided below (for the purpose of invoicing the registration fee).

The registration fee (EUR 500) shall be transferred to one of the DFB's accounts, following receipt of the invoice issued by the DFB. To enable the DFB to issue said invoice, please fill in the data requested below. In the event that the invoicing address is different from the below postal address, please advise accordingly. If the Intermediary has been registered already, no additional data need to be filled in.

Firm/company	
Full name	
Street, no.	
Zip code	
Town/city	
Email	
Tax ID no.	
VAT ID no. (if applicable)	

If the Intermediary wishes their contact details to be published on the DFB website, they may contact Spielervermittlung@dfb.de

Place ....

Date ....

Signature ....

Mandate for transfer

(In this case, the agent has a mandate to conduct a transfer of the player to the English Premier League and Championship, the Turkish Süper Lig, and America's Major League Soccer. Furthermore, it is between the agent seeking to make a deal, and the full-time agent of the player. As discussed in Chapter 7, mandates can either be an agent–player or an agent–agent agreement, depending on what is stated in the initial Representation Contract. The following example is relatively concise, and mandates can be longer than this, but do not have to be.)

INTERMEDIATION CONTRACT

This Contract is between

Company of the Intermediary: ....
Intermediary name: ....
Intermediary number: ....
Address: ....

Onwards 'the Intermediary'

Company of the Agent: ....
Agent name: ....
Intermediary number: ....
Address: ....

Onwards 'the Agent'

It is hereby agreed as follows:

1   Preamble
    The Agent represents exclusively the interests of the
    professional football player   ....
    who currently plays for ....
    ('the Player'), with regards to the negotiation or
    renegotiation of a Contract to a football club ('the
    Transfer').

2.   Authorisation
2.1 The Agent authorises the Intermediary to represent
    the Player for the following football clubs ('the Clubs'):

• All Clubs in the English Premier League and
  Championship (First and Second Division)
• All Clubs in the Süper Lig of Turkey (First Division)
• All Clubs in the Major League Soccer of the United
  States of America

2.2 The Intermediary is authorised to initiate and direct
    discussions with the Clubs and to negotiate a Transfer
    for the Player to one of the Clubs. The Intermediary
    must inform the Agent of every discussion and
    negotiation.

2.3 The Intermediary has the right to make a final decision,
    only with the previous consent of the Agent, with

regards to an agreement for a Transfer of the Player to a Club.

2.4 Every proposal, agreement and contract issued by the Player, the Club or the Intermediary must be presented to the Agent. For the Transfer to be valid, the approval of the Player and the Agent is required.

2.5 The Contract shall take effect on ....
and will terminate on ....
without notice.

3. Remuneration
The Intermediary and the Agent agree to split the negotiated commission for the Transfer of the Player as follows:
- 50% for the Intermediary
- 50% for the Agent

4. Termination
The Contract shall be automatically terminated with immediate effect if the Intermediary's Registration expires during the term of the Contract and the Intermediary does not renew his Registration within 14 days of being requested to do so in writing by the Player.

5. Disputes
Any dispute arising from or related to the present Contract will be submitted exclusively to the Court

of Arbitration for Sport in Lausanne, Switzerland, and resolved definitively in accordance with the Code of Sports-Related Arbitration.

6. Governing Law
    The Contract and any non-contractual obligation arising out of or in connection to it are governed by and shall be construed in accordance with the laws of England and Wales and subject to Clause 5 above. The parties hereby submit to the exclusive jurisdiction of the courts of England and Wales.

7. Final Notes
7.1 In case any of the articles in the Contract are ineffective or inapplicable, the remaining articles will not be affected. The contracting parties agree to solve the issues that arise in the best way possible and in good faith to provide a valid article that is as similar as possible to the ineffective article.

7.2 This Contract will be signed in two copies. Copies will be as follows:
    1. Agent
    2. Intermediary

Date: ....

Intermediary (print name): ....
(signature): ....

Agent (print name): ....
(signature): ....

Premier League Employment Contract

(This is an example of Schedule 2 of a Premier League Employment Contract. This part of the agreement is where aspects like length of deal and salary are to be found, and where bonuses and performance-based clauses are stated.)

Schedule 2

Player's name: ....

Supplemental Provisions and Employment Rights Act 1996

The following provisions shall apply to supplement the provisions of this contract and the information as set out herein in order to comply with the requirements of Part 1 of the Employment Rights Act 1996.

1. The Player's employment with the Club began on:

    ....

2. The date of termination of this contract is: ....

    ....

3. No employment with a previous employer shall count as part of the Player's continuous period of employment hereunder.

4. The Player's hours of work are such as the Club may from time to time reasonably require of him to carry out his duties and the Player shall not be entitled to

any additional remuneration for work done outside normal working hours.

5. The place of employment shall be at the Club's ground and training ground, but the Club shall be entitled to require the Player to play and to undertake his duties hereunder at any other place throughout the world.

6. No contracting-out certificate pursuant to the Pensions Scheme Act 1993 is in force in respect of the Player's employment under this contract.

7. The Professional Footballers' Pension Scheme

    7.1 Immediately on signing this contract, the Player shall:

        7.1.1   be automatically enrolled as,

        7.1.2   or continue to be

    a member of the 2011 Section of the Professional Footballers' Pension Scheme ('the Scheme'), and shall remain so during the continuance of his employment hereunder unless he:

    7.1.3 notifies the Scheme Administrator in writing that he wishes to opt out of the Scheme;

    7.1.4 has previously registered with HM Revenue & Customs for Fixed or Enhanced Protection; or

    7.1.5 is otherwise ineligible for membership of the Scheme in accordance with the terms of the Scheme's definitive trust deed and rules as amended from time to time.

    7.2 For as long as the Player remains a member of the 2011 Section, an annual contribution (funded by the levy on transfer fees) will be paid into the Scheme for the benefit of the Player. The annual contribution shall be £5,208 or such other amount as determined by the Trustees of the Scheme from time to time.

7.3 The Player shall not be required to contribute to the 2011 Section but may elect to contribute such amount as he notifies to the Scheme Administrator in writing. Where a Player decides to contribute to the 2011 Section he can agree with his Club and the Scheme Administrator for the contribution to be made through a salary sacrifice arrangement.

7.4 Where, by virtue of previous membership of the Scheme, the Player has built up benefits under its Cash Section and/or Income Section, those benefits are frozen and will be revalued until his retirement from the Scheme. The Player shall be entitled to such benefits (including death benefits) from each section of the Scheme in which he has participated on such conditions as are set out in the Scheme's definitive trust deed and rules as amended from time to time.

7.5 The Player further agrees that the Club may disclose his name, address, gender, date of birth, National Insurance number, salary information, and dates of commencement and termination of employment to the League and the administrators of the Scheme for the purposes of facilitating the administration of the Scheme.

8. Remuneration

The Player's remuneration shall be:

8.1 Basic wage:

£ per week/per annum payable by monthly instalments in arrears from .... to ....

£ per week/per annum payable by monthly instalments in arrears from .... to ....

£ per week/per annum payable by monthly instalments in arrears from .... to ....

£ per week/per annum payable by monthly instalments in arrears from .... to ....

£ per week/per annum payable by monthly instalments in arrears from .... to ....

    8.2 Such of the bonuses and incentives as the Player shall be entitled to receive under the terms of the Club's bonus and incentive scheme as are set out below/a copy of which is annexed hereto:

....

    8.3 Any other payments as follows:

....

9.   Insurances (if any) maintained for the benefit of the Player subject to the terms and conditions thereof during currency of this contract, the premiums of which are paid by the Club.

    Nature of policy: Amount:

    ....

10. Benefits (if any) to be provided to the Player during the currency of this contract:

....
....
....

11. The Player's normal retirement age is 35 years.

12. The terms and conditions of this contract form part of a number of collective agreements between the Club (through the League) and the Player (through the PFA) affecting the Player's employment, and full details thereof are set out in the Code of Practice.

13. (If applicable) The following provisions which are additional or supplemental to those set out in Clause 4 have been agreed between the Club and the Player as referred to in Clause 4.11 [found in Schedule 1]:

....
....
....

14. Any other provisions:

....
....
....

SIGNED by the Player: ....
in the presence of: ....
Witness signature: ....
Address: ....
Occupation: ....

SIGNED by the Player's parent or guardian
(if the player is under 18):

....
in the presence of: ....
Witness signature: ....
Address: ....
Occupation: ....

SIGNED by (name): ....

for and on behalf of the Club in the presence of:

....

Witness signature: ....

Address: ....

Occupation: ....

Did the Player use the services

of an Intermediary?   yes/no

If yes, name of Intermediary: ....

Signature of Intermediary: ....

Did the Club use the services of an Intermediary?   yes/no

If yes, name of Intermediary: ....

Signature of Intermediary: ....

Marketing deal

(The following contract covers the most important parts discussed in Chapter 10. Although these contracts will likely include more legal definitions and technical jargon from the company, the basics are covered. This particular example is that of a headphones company.)

Talent: ....

Lender: ....

Effective date: ....

Company: ....

Licensed IP:

The name, likeness, image, or digitized image, video or film portrayal, photograph, biography, voice and endorsement of Talent, including any autograph, initials, facsimile signature, nickname, symbol or other means of endorsement or identification.

Products:

Headphones, earphones, speakers and other audio products and accessories (as are agreed between the parties from time to time) that are branded as ....

Term:

A period of two (2) years beginning on the date of full execution of this Talent Agreement by all parties; provided that any Content captured from a Shoot may be used until the later of the end of the Term or six months from date of first use (provided such Content is initially used during the Term); provided, further, that any results of Talent's services hereunder (including the Content) may be used in perpetuity for internal and/or archival purposes, editorial purposes and other non-advertising purposes (such as, without limitation, in advertising awards competitions, film festivals, retrospectives and archival and/or historical sections of Company's websites and social media pages). Each consecutive twelve (12) month period commencing on the date of mutual execution of this Talent Agreement during the Term is referred to herein as a 'Contract Year'.

Payment/Payment Terms:
As full and complete compensation for any and all personal services rendered and the grant of rights herein, Company will pay Lender an annual fee for each Contract Year equal to .... (the 'Annual Compensation'), in quarterly payments during the Contract Year, to be invoiced in arrears. All payments of the Annual Compensation will be made within forty-five (45) days of receipt by Company of Lender's proper invoice therefor in accordance with Company's instructions.

Performance Bonuses:
In the event that Talent achieves any of the following, Company shall pay to Lender a Bonus Payment (a 'Bonus') in the amount described below in respect of each such achievement, such Bonus payable no more than once per

Contract Year. Lender shall invoice Company for such Bonus within thirty (30) days of the closing of achievement and Company will pay such Bonus within forty-five (45) days of receipt of Lender's proper invoice therefor, in accordance with Company's instructions.

Achievement Bonus:
Premier League Winner: £ ....
Champions League Winner (on pitch): £ ....
Premier League Player of the Year: £ ....
Ballon d'Or: £ ....
UEFA Euro 2020 Winner: £ ....
UEFA Euro 2020 Player of Tournament: £ ....

Territory: ....

Marketing Obligations:
Lender will cause Talent to endorse the Products and provide other marketing support for the benefit of the Company pursuant to a plan developed by the parties, including promotional appearances, photographic/film/ voice shoots and similar activities; which plan shall include, at a minimum, the following marketing support services:

• Talent shall participate in two (2) full photograph/film/ voice shoot days (6 hours each) per Contract Year, on such dates and locations as otherwise mutually agreed by the Parties (collectively, 'the Shoots').
• Wear, when appropriate, the Products (to be provided by Company).

- Coordinated social messaging through Talent's social media channels as mutually agreed upon between the parties hereto across all of Talent's social media platforms (i.e. Facebook, Instagram, Twitter) with Product (approximately one post per month across all channels); tagging of official channels will be coordinated on request of Company. During campaigns, social media post frequency will increase to two (2) posts per month across all channels. Company social media accounts may retweet and/or repost Talent's social media messages, and may promote and/or whitelist Talent's social media messages on all social media platforms including Facebook and Twitter.

- One (1) promotional appearance per Contract Year of at least four (4) hours. Each promotional appearance may include private and public events or clinics with Company's customers or consumers. At any such promotional appearance, Talent will pose for a reasonable number of photographs and privately sign a reasonable amount of autographs. Company will determine the dates, times and locations for any personal appearances subject to consultation with and the prior approval of Lender based upon Talent's prior personal, professional and commercial commitments, and provided that Talent will treat Company no less favorably than their other commercial commitments in terms of availability.

If Talent is required to travel for the purpose of attending a Shoot or an appearance, Company shall pay for actual and reasonable business-class travel and premium lodging expenses in accordance with Company's Travel Policy for Suppliers. All Talent's services and the results and proceeds of the services rendered and/or created hereunder (including, without limitation, any commercials, photographs, marketing or promotional materials, films, recordings, and any Shoot assets) shall be referred to herein as 'Content'.

Company Obligations:
After the beginning of the Term, Company shall provide a reasonable amount of a selection of its newest and/or custom Products, as designed by Company, to Talent for their own use, or (at Talent's discretion) for certain individuals such as Talent's coaches and other athletes (the retail value of such Products to be approximately $5,000 each Contract Year during the Term).

Exclusivity Restrictions:
Lender agrees that, during the Term, neither Lender nor Talent will use or grant any licence or rights to any other party in the Licensed IP or any portion thereof in any way, manner or form in connection with the manufacture, distribution, marketing, promotion and/or sale of headphones, earphones, speakers and other audio products and accessories. Further, Lender agrees that Talent shall not wear or display any other brand of headphones or earphones in public during the Term.

Termination:
A party may immediately terminate this Talent Agreement if the other party is in material breach of this Talent

Agreement and that party fails to cure that breach within thirty (30) days after receiving written notice of breach from the non-breaching party. Further, Company may, in its opinion, deem Lender to be in material breach of this Talent Agreement and immediately suspend its performance, including, but not limited to, payment of any compensation, or terminate this Talent Agreement immediately if:

(i)   Talent engages in Negative Behavior or is charged with a felony during the Term; or

(ii) Talent (a) fails to remain on the active roster (excluding the injured list) of ....
      or other UEFA team and the ....
      national team for any continuous ninety (90) day period during the Term; or (b) incurs an injury, suffers an illness or develops a medical condition (other than resulting from illegal or illicit drug use) that prevents Talent from playing professional soccer for a continuous period of more than ninety (90) days.

'Negative Behavior' means any action or statement by Talent that brings Talent into public disrepute, contempt, scandal or ridicule, or that shocks or offends the community or any group or class thereof, or that reflects unfavorably on Company, including making any or authorizing any statements in derogation of Company or its brand or its products which become or are made known to the public.

Signed by: ....

Duly authorised for and on behalf of: ....

Dated: ....

Signed by: ....

Duly authorised for and on behalf of: ....

Dated: ....

_____

CONCLUSION

Football agency is a tough business that requires you to be hard-working, flexible and hungry for success – it demands sacrifice and diligence from the start. At first, this can seem daunting and unattainable, but at the same time the challenges you face should act as greater motivation. No profession allows you to rise to the top with immediate effect, and this industry is no different. Nevertheless, with the increased professionalisation of football and intermediaries, there is every possibility that you can leave your mark on the game. Whilst this job is certainly competitive, there is no shortage of football players to represent, and the future will only pave the way for a greater role for agents.

There is no hiding from the hard work and number of hours needed to succeed in this business, but at the same time one must not neglect the perks of the job. Being involved in the world's most popular sport and mixing with football players often entitles you to unforgettable experiences across the globe that are unparalleled in the majority of other industries. Additionally, the money in football can allow you to be well remunerated throughout your career.

However, although money is a key consideration, it cannot be the aspect of the job that motivates you from the outset. As in nearly all professions, when starting out, the money simply isn't there, as experience and clients will be lacking. This is why perseverance and passion have to be characteristics that you possess – having qualities such as these gives you the greatest chance at success.

Of paramount importance is not giving up. If you decide to embark on a career in football agency, it will be difficult and at times feel impossible – but by working hard and working smart, there is nothing stopping you from achieving the goals you have set yourself.

SOCIAL MEDIA

Get in touch for more information and advice on becoming a football agent! Don't forget to keep up to date with our teaching and seminar events worldwide.

Website: www.footballagenteduation.com
LinkedIn: Football Agent Education
Instagram: @footballagenteducation
Facebook: Football Agent Education
Twitter: @education_agent